7 Steps to Overcoming Adversity & Transforming your Life

Hyacinth J Myers

Don't let your story
define you!

Love
Hyacinth
x

30/5/19

This First Edition is Published by

Soul Conscious Creations Ltd in April 2019

© Copyright 2019, Hyacinth J Myers

ISBN: 978-1-9160730-0-5

Cover Photo: Lee Townsend, Photographer www.leetownsend.co.uk

www.soulconsciouscreations.com

www.hyacinthmyers.com

Printed by Book Printing UK, Peterborough PE2 9B

About the Author

Hyacinth is a forty-seven year old dual heritage mother of two Sons. She is a graduate and was born and has lived most of her life in Hackney, London when not living in Plymouth or Birmingham (UK). She is a Creative woman who still cannot define her title and multiple business owner. She does not fit into any box. Hyacinth is also Founder/ Managing Director of Soul Conscious Creations offering her Signature (7 Step 7 Week) course, Workshops and Monthly Sister Circle based on her Empower 7 Women's Personal Development Programme. She uses her Intuitive Coaching/ Mentoring skills and Holistic Therapies to help heal past adversities by empowering women to create their life by Design, acknowledging, reflecting, embracing and supporting them to work through their personal story. She specialises in Women over thirty who are Stuck or at a Crossroads in their life.

She is also an Award-Winning Jewellery designer/ maker, International Speaker, Artist, Photographer, Published Writer (celebrating twenty-three years) and Qualified Holistic Therapist specialising in Reiki and Indian Head Massage at present. Her hobbies include Personal/ Spiritual (interfaith) development, Advanced Learning and Training (over 25+ years in FE), Spending time with her Children/ Family, Reading, Travel, Landscape Photography and Visiting places of interest.

This year celebrating thirty years, she has been an avid Community worker in various fields including Children and Young people in Adventure Playgrounds and Community centres, Prison Visitor, Sexual health and HIV Prevention Team leader, Arts Ambassador, Campaigner and Magazine Panel Member for Bliss The Premature baby Charity, Various Charity Committee Member roles and Steering groups as well as more recently for HiP (Hackney's Independent Parent's Forum for Parents of Children with Special Educational Needs and Disabilities). In March 2018 she received a *Divas of Colour* **"Woman of Honour"** Award for her Service to community which was wonderful recognition and one of her proudest moments.

Too many women hide their story like she did for years for fear of judgement, blame, embarrassment. She believed she was broken but has come to realise that her story helps inspire others and motivates them to reach for their dreams regardless. Her vision is to Empower thousands of women to heal and in turn they will empower others creating a mass global movement. She doesn't want to create Followers but empower women to be Leaders.

On 30th of March 2017, EMPOWER 7 the Programme was launched offering Workshops for Women who were struggling to Overcome Adversity and Trauma. This was born out of her own personal experiences and is a program that uses meditation, reflective exercises, Journaling, Group discussions and Creative activities to begin or accelerate a journey of self-discovery and can be delivered as a series of stand-alone workshops or as a complete Programme either in a Group or 1-2-1. Her message/motto is simple *"You don't have to be a victim of your circumstances, you can be Soul Conscious Creators of your Future".*

For more information Please Contact

Web
www.soulconsciouscreations.com
www.hyacinthmyers.com

Social media
Instagram- @empower__7
Facebook- @hyacinthjmyers
LinkedIn- @HyacinthMyers
Twitter- @hyacinthjmyers

Email
soulcc@live.co.uk
Mobile
(+44) 7456 713 830

Thank You/ Acknowledgements

I want to Thank first and foremost our Creator and the Universe for always having my back.

To my Mother Linda whose unconditional love, support and practical help (at times daily) has propelled me to where I am now.

My son's Okera and Kwame for supporting and being good children generally, teaching me as well as testing me in every aspect possible whilst achieving and excelling despite their own adversities. Thanks to my sister Denise for always being there regardless.

My Life Partner of nine years Franklin Burton for putting up with the ups and downs of an Aquarian woman whilst I worked way too much and haven't seen him as much as I want to. Also for the practical support and discussions birthing new ideas too many to follow through.

My friends especially Talibah, Karen, Joy Francis, Jennifer Beaumont-Whyte, Felicia (being the wheels to give me the practical help at times especially Launch) as well as new friends who believed in the vision (many who have contributed Quotes). My USA Champion Mr Nautech (Richard) for encouraging me from the year 2000 to reach for the stars and been supportive in so much without judgement.

Thank You Mr Sukhi Wahiwala (my first Business Mentor who believed in me even when I didn't believe in myself). You have pushed me to be my best and I appreciate you. And my Project Management Coach/ Mentor Serena for helping me to manifest this dream as well as Business Adviser from East London Business Place.

Local Artist and Community empower woman (Up Your Street) Gillian Lawrence for allowing me step up by supporting from the beginning and celebrating me as a local Champion in the Exhibition. (The piece hangs proudly on my kitchen wall)
Thank You DJ Mary Katherine and Producer Ian for allowing me a platform to shine on East London radio as a newbie before EMPOWER 7 launched and twice since and continued support and Gillian for the introduction.

My friend and neighbour International multi-talented Musician, Singer/ Songwriter Kodjovi Kush for your support and entertainment at events.

My friend Jennifer Beckford for wonderful Cakes at events and support. You went above and beyond at my Launch event in 2017.

My friend and trusted Holistic Therapist Howard who has taken me through so much, so I was healed and ready to be of great service to other women in this world and my meditation group.

Thank You Livingston and Brenda of MLB Learning Solutions who allow me to use space and constantly encourage me to step forward.

As well as all my Ladies who Latte groups for continued support and all the women who have been there in one way or another. You are all appreciated!

Last but no means least, to those I have never met who are tied to my DNA in one way or another, grandads and grandmothers, ancestors and angels, everyone here or in spirit who guide me daily. Without all of you, the love and support, none of this would be possible.

And Thank you reader for taking a chance with this book whilst being courageous enough to do the inner work of reflection needed for you to thrive and live your life on purpose! You always have a choice!

You are seen!

You are loved!

And although I don't know you personally.....Our ultimate journey as humans is to reawaken all of the self on a bigger and better scale.

Welcome to the start or continuation of your journey….
Love and Blessings always
With love and light

Hyacinth x

P.S. **In the spirit of Paying it Forward 10% of book sales will be donated to various Charities/ Organisations.**
Details will be published on the website regularly.

Dedication

To my loved ones who have left this earthly realm over with the Ancestors in Spirit.

My 23 day old baby Shaka born at 23 weeks and twin (we loved you dearly). Thank You for teaching me to be strong and what it's like to love so deeply and grieve so quickly.

My Dad Winston who although we only developed a relationship when I was 21 didn't mean we weren't close. I'm glad I forgave you for not being present in my life. Love you dad!

My close Family friend Theophilus aka Steve who was like a Dad to me when I didn't know my dad especially and after. Thanks Violet, Talibah and family for sharing him with me!

My close friend Ricardo. You made me promise to dedicate my first book to you.
Other friend's I have lost including, Rest in Paradise!

CONTENTS

Introduction

Introduction

Greetings Beautiful Souls,

I hope this book finds you in the best of health and happiness. If it doesn't my hope and wish for you is that it soon will.

In life we go through Adversity/ Challenges/ Problems and for some of us it's more than others. It can feel as if something is wrong with us and is often reinforced by people saying things like *I have bad luck*. When I talk about adversity, I mean serious challenges or traumas not the run of the mill challenges we have throughout life.

As a child and into Adulthood I was very closed off and hid what I deemed to be the broken pieces of my life. I grew up in one of the poorest Boroughs in London at the time which was Hackney. I lived on a notorious estate and in a property where domestic violence occurred. It created a fear in me and withdrawal as a highly sensitive child with a strong sense of injustice. The eldest of four and an older child will resonate with this because your sense of responsibility for everyone is high. For many years I internalized this trauma and used Poetry, Art and Writing as an escape. These were my creative outlets and my way to express as I never told anyone whilst we lived there. These are now my blessings!

Unspoken trauma and Silences can be just as damaging as psychologists now know. As I aged and became a young woman, I seemed to attract negative situations and unhealthy relationships with boyfriend's though male friendships flourished and were platonic with a huge element of protection for me as well as mutual respect and understanding.

Enduring Rape, Verbal abuse, Gaslighting, Sexual Assault, Single parenthood, a Complicated Twin pregnancy and then Child death (Neonatal) on top of having one child who was diagnosed with Depression at eleven years old and the other with Anxiety, Cognitive/ Processing difficulties and other Special Educational Needs and Disabilities I'd say I have overcome a lot. Needless, to say, I think I'm more than qualified in writing about adversity and in creating the EMPOWER 7 programme.

Out of Adversity great things happen. Either you become stuck (or like myself and many others) you grow. It teaches you something. You learn about another part of yourself you didn't know or resurface what was hidden or forgotten. Don't get me wrong, I spent many years feeling sorry for myself but I also gave back to community as a way of self healing and remembering there are always others who are worse off. In fact this year I am celebrating giving back thirty years of service to Community.

This book is a culmination of my experiences, insights, tools and tips learnt over my forty plus years of life. I hope you find it useful and please feel free to email your comments/ feedback/ stories to me. I will read them all personally unless I receive thousands. I hope to make a difference in many lives by sharing all that I have as my purpose is to inspire and empower women (especially) to live a life by Design regardless of their circumstances or story. We are all here for a wonderful god given reason and it is my mission to impact thousands of Women's lives globally so in turn they can do the same. My mission is to create a tribe of Leaders *not* Followers and I know that all of our Personal/ Spiritual journeys are as individual as our fingerprints are, so listen to your intuition whilst reading this book and see what resonates.

My wish for you is to have an open mind and read this knowing that there are many of us out there working to empower, nurture and support women genuinely, authentically and with great integrity for your highest and greatest good.

This book is laid out in 7 chapters and each chapter covers a module in the EMPOWER 7 Women's personal development programme. This is what makes up the 7 Steps. It will cover personal stories, tools, tips that I have discovered with relevance, a Quote from an amazing Woman I know, An affirmation and a quick Task at the end. My aim is that you learn whilst on this reading journey more about yourself and develop insights.

So sit back, grab a notepad (if you are inclined) and welcome to the start of a more reflective journey, and remember if parts are hard to deal with don't stop, breakthrough and know you deserve to move forward just as much as the next woman.

I'll see you on the other side. If you want to stay the same then put this book back down but if you want to change your story then open up and let's begin…...

Step One

Embrace your life

" Never give up, Keep going always "
(Denise Myers, Carer and Buddha Enthusiast)

EMBRACE Yourself and the Life you have. Where you have been? Where you are? and Where you are going? Embrace unconditionally. Everything happens for a reason so let's try to find the Positive!

" Find Acceptance in where you are right now. Acceptance is the first point in being able to heal and move forward "
(Sherese Thomas- Coach and Founder of the Mind Haven)

You are not your past!! If anyone had ever told me I would view my childhood experiences as a blessing, I would have been really insulted. How could I grow up in a house where (although I didn't witness the domestic violence in front of me) I was terrorized by the screams and pleas to stop from my mother whilst late at night in bed and always wondering if she would be alive the next day. I heard the awful threats my step dad made. Now I think those adversities only helped to make me stronger and more resilient even with a bit of PTSD and years in private therapy thrown in. I am now grateful for everything. I give thanks I know that my story has been helping others even though family members are not best pleased. As a child growing up in a house of domestic violence in an estate in Hackney during the 1970s and 80s, I was born into a family of a White English mother and Jamaican father and stepfather.

Mum had four children, was estranged from her family (mother died when she was eighteen) with no real close friends who weren't being abused themselves. I can understand now as an adult why she stayed. We left the family home when I was sixteen and my youngest sibling was eleven years old to go into a woman's Refuge for a few days before moving out of the borough into a temporary house in neighbouring Waltham Forest.

Our childhood home environment was very disempowering for my mum, myself and siblings. Verbal Abuse towards my mum (sometimes daily) and constantly reinforcing we weren't good enough and wouldn't amount to much was not a good start. I believe my mum's spirit was broken and worn out. Apparently, the domestic violence and aggression was only going on for six years but it felt like my whole childhood quite honestly because of the lasting impact.

During this difficult (and I would go as far to say traumatic)

2

childhood, I found my own way of empowering myself as I would later discover. That was the pen and paper writing fantasy escape stories and poems as much as I could as well as becoming immersed in Art. Often fantasizing about a different life, my real dad saving us and the normality of family life I perceived everyone to have.

Our environment can either empower or disempower us but as we know it is all down to perception. *Is the glass half full or half empty as the analogy goes?* It is in these places we find our passions. I wasn't really allowed out much but when I was the local adventure playground was where my passion for helping others and Community began. I started volunteering as a fifteen year old before getting paid work with Hackney Council at the age of seventeen nearly eighteen. I think I always knew to beware of my thoughts as I would look for other situations where I could help others and empower them. I always thought there must be someone worse off than us and where we lived there most certainly was.

So what can we learn at life's various stages?
To sum it up.....a hell of a lot. If we try and disconnect all the emotions of the situations and look at each individually with the lessons they have taught us then we will see clearly. As I was *in* the situation, it was a minefield and unfortunately because I was so emotional I always found struggle hard to navigate. I searched the adults around me I can honestly say I didn't have any role models I

aspired to be. I had no grandparents, no aunties I knew, no cousins, no uncles and thought when I grew up I wanted a big close family who didn't use violence and abuse to control others, who weren't hypercritical and empowered me to achieve more than the hand we were dealt. I had a few people I had admired such as a close family friend who helped us get into the women's refuge and generally has been a great supporter to me over the years while going to university and who is still in my life now even though she is in her seventies.

In regard to our life situation, challenges and happy achievements, these all teach us something. It's learning what the something is, that is the key to life and unlocking our own self-mastery.

Family patterns influence us much more than your average person realises. If you come from a 'so-called' dysfunctional family it's estimated you will more than likely go on to create that as a pattern when thinking about psychology or what drives human behaviour, Societies and ultimately Countries. My family pattern was growing up with step father as my parents split when I was a toddler. My dad had a new family but it turns out to be one where my half brothers and sisters are either older, younger or literally the same age within months. According to statistics I had a much higher than average chance of also living in an estate in poverty with absent fathers or lone parent and a full-time mother with the odd low paying part-time job. From as far back as I can remember I had it in my head 'no way' and knew that at the very least, happiness was my birthright if nothing else. I love my mum dearly. She has sacrificed her whole life for us. Being abandoned by her father and family. Losing her mother to cancer at the age of eighteen and everything in-between she has never said as we are the children and she's the adult still to this day. But your family ideas about you are not yours.

So although family patterns do influence us more than we realise, they don't make us. The things that helped me to continue these patterns were not my environment but my negative critical voice that stayed with me for many more years. That is a difference between what changes and what stays the same. Two people can have the same awful experience occur but respond so very differently and as children we are very impressionable.

So think about the family patterns you have (Childhood and now) and situations/ experiences that you may need to embrace in your life. In 2006 I became a single mother for the second time (this time during pregnancy). Apart from being devastated, I also had no choice but to embrace it. At the time I was chastising myself for being so stupid. Here I was struggling as a single mum with a seven year old boy after myself and his dad (my fiance) split up when he was six months old after five years and here I was pregnant again by a man nine years younger then me and only after a five month relationship. He wasn't interested in taking responsibility and was harassing/ threatening me daily about getting an abortion. I had already taken the Morning After Pill and had tests that said pregnancy was negative so was in a state of shock and horror now not only finding out I was pregnant, but that it was twins. Could things get any worse? and yes they did. The negative voice twenty-four hours a day silently wishing for this to be a dream asking how an otherwise sensible and responsible woman could get herself in this position played over and over. And as soon as the first trimester started so did the continuous bleeding, threatened miscarriage, emergency visits to Accident and Emergency, unsympathetic staff as I'd booked the termination but cancelled, and the hospital were not best pleased telling me how much money I had cost the NHS. It felt like the odds were against me. Fast forward and at twenty-three weeks (one week before I was six months pregnant) I had a sudden spontaneous birth and twin boys were born weighing one pound ten ounces and one pound two ounces. Needing resuscitation and taken immediately to intensive care this was the worst I could imagine or experience. My negative critical voice said "well this is your punishment for being so foolish...well done!!". My state of mind was not good and to make matters worse my youngest boy Shaka died at the age of twenty-three days old. Always remember you are not your thoughts.

So when negative situations occur we need to be in the company of positive people in order to be supported to grow. I could have quite easily given up because I wasn't tired, I was mentally exhausted then and it crossed my mind daily. I cried more than I think I ever have and though on the outside I seemed calm, centred and handling it well, I wasn't. I was beating myself up mentally daily for knowing better. I was replaying some of the conversations I'd had with other parents on the ward. Only a few were brave enough to ask where the father was while others gave disappointing fake smiles just as the consultant did at my local hospital I had moved from. He had the cheek to enter the appointment I had booked one and a half hours late when I was nearly five months pregnant and asked me where the father was because I attended the appointment alone. He then chuckled as he asked "*Did he run off because you're having twins?*" I said yes and burst into tears then left and vowed never to go back and left the hospital permanently. How unprofessional and insensitive but I guess he was saying what others were thinking. I was not going to give birth there. Where was the professionalism and compassion? Long gone I thought. And I didn't feel safe with them so after a dream and researching hospitals specialising in premature birth I told my doctor I wasn't going back. I spoke to a number of family members and friends determined I would change hospitals because of the lack of overall care and feeling really ill (almost poisoned) with no tests being carried out, being fobbed off and not listening. One friend who was always (and still is) so positive, told me changing hospital would be better. I was so undecided and in fear. Most of the people around me amplified that with the '*what if..?'* and then the worst case scenario. Thank God for her. I researched hospitals spoke to my also fear ridden and reluctant doctor who didn't want me to change but told him I wouldn't attend appointments because they weren't looking after me anyway and I would deliver the twins myself at home if I had to. He agreed and within two weeks I transfered to University College London Hospital in Euston (my choice) and went into early labour two weeks later. I delivered my twins and was told my care was very poor before and also diagnosed with septicemia which had also been in my blood long enough to cross over in the womb to the twins who had to fight this life-threatening situation. I actually was poisoned.

So why bother tell you all this?

Because in all situations in life (especially the difficult and challenging ones) we must embrace it. Only when we do that, we take control and grow through adversity. In order to prosper we must grow on all levels.

Dealing effectively with negative people especially during a tough time is probably one of the hardest things to conquer. I found it very hard and even in positive situations too.

Whatever you are going through in life there will always be others who are waiting in the wings to moan, complain, put doubts in your head (even if there were none before) and well and truly put you on the path to the helpless mentality. Don't let them! It's getting to grips with this that takes time. When someone says you can't, it's a

8

complete joy when internally you say 'I can'. Breathe it out and move on. Sometimes people are negative for their own reasons. Maybe childhood issues, past relationship hurts jealousy or annoyance are factors. Whatever it is you really shouldn't take too much time out wondering why. It's not your problem. Counteracting the negative statements is hard enough. They say for every negative comment made to you sixteen or seventeen positive ones need to be replaced to counteract that. If for some reason the negative person is prominent in your life, it may be a case of removing yourself more from that relationship or contacting less. I had to do this personally myself and although probably the hardest part of my personal development journey, it has definitely proved the most fruitful.

So how can we look at every situation positively many people ask? The answer is simple.....focus on the positive. Regardless of the situation see it as a test to do your best, learn and take one day at a time. In our darkest hours it is so hard to see the light at the end of the tunnel but embracing the situation means that although it is not something pleasurable, you really are on the journey to get through it with minimal damage to your health, mental health and peace of mind.

After we left the family home to go into a women's refuge we could have stayed in the victim mentality. What we had to do (myself, mum, and siblings) was to embrace it. For us we wanted a new start, a new life, a peace I don't remember ever having. I wanted the fear and terror i experienced as a child to end. I wanted my mum happy. Truly happy like I saw others. I wanted to be carefree but I also wanted all of my books, toys stories, poems, clothes and everything else we had to leave behind. You see that was our sacrifice. Mum packed two carrier bags and the clothes on our backs when we left. It was a sudden departure and that was it. Imagine two carrier bags of four people's lives. I felt it was hugely unfair, unjust and such an infringement on our basic human rights. Fast forward thirty years (this year) and I have used these experiences to work with other women I am coaching and mentoring to overcome their story. It's important to make sure that regardless of the situation you make it as positive as possible after it has occurred if not during the time. **What do you need to embrace?** I'll get you to think about this a few times throughout this chapter.

Another important thing to do throughout life is to celebrate and recreate your best times. We live in a fast-paced society where we rarely stop and celebrate our achievements. So often we continue on, telling a few close friends and family about them which is such a shame. I used to do it myself. I used to be very hard on myself and set the bar so high I'd never expect no one else to have or achieve and then take it for granted as I was meant to achieve it. No celebration was needed but it is these times of achievements that remembering helps to boost your morale and remind you that you aren't a failure. In our darkest hours or when we feel a bit tired and get fed up it's great to have a reminder. Why not have a wipe clean board where you can write down your achievements or little blessings/ miracles for the month as a constant reminder! I do this myself and then type it up and hang it where I can see it. You'll notice a pattern of more (the lists growing bigger) so it encourages you to count your blessings constantly.

Everything happens for a reason or so we keep being told so count your blessings. *Do you believe that?* I honestly do! I think when you get to a certain age and have many experiences. good and bad, if you have what they call a growth mindset you know there is some higher purpose or reason as to why this has happened.

When I was in my early twenties either twenty-one or twenty-two, I remember using a shortcut I'd always used through my local cemetery. It wasn't enclosed not dark or spooky and was often busy with people day and night. It was broad daylight about lunchtime I recall it vividly. I was wearing my earphones (something I've never done since) and thinking about a journey I was about to make to Birmingham. In the distance I could hear footsteps behind me and running but as I said it was busy so no need to be alarmed. As the running neared I remember getting that feeling like something wasn't right and my heart started racing. All I felt was someone run their hand up my leg touch my private area and run off. The speed at which it happened was shocking.

So quick I screamed a man and woman walking towards me shouted at a man who all could see was the back of him. I remember feeling so invaded I went straight to the police station right near the cemetery and remember how unsympathetic and rude the police were to me. They recorded it as a sexual assault talked about my short skirt and one week later the same person (I believe) as he was in the same clothes with the same build raped a woman in the same cemetery. My partner at the time (who I was going to see) was very unsympathetic too and I remember the blame others were putting on me. Little did they know I had already been raped a few years previous and hadn't told any of them for the same reasons because too many people blame the woman.

So why tell you all this?

Well not for any sympathy. My stories, adversities and life experiences have all made me into the woman I am today. Moreover so you know that regardless of the situation, there is always a reason or something to learn. I believe my reason at that time during the cemetery incident, was to drive home the fact that I needed to be much more alert and streetwise. I used to float around walking almost aimlessly at times which I later found out to be dangerous as male predators were always looking out for vulnerable young girls to take advantage of. The other thing it taught me was to be compassionate to women who have experienced sexual assault and violence and one step further was to try to understand the mind of a sex offender when I decided to work for four years voluntary with lifers in prison disowned by their family for their sexual offences as part of my own healing journey. My boundary and cut-off point was that although I didn't have any children of my own then I wasn't able to bring myself to work with people who had committed acts against children. I also use these negative and traumatic experiences to work with women who are stuck in their story by Coaching and Mentoring them through by openly sharing my story and why they need to use this as a stepping stone rather than a full stop. Now experiences like this I even count as blessings for what they have taught me.

There are so many reasons why we need to overcome loss but why is it that so many are stuck in the pain of it and seem to just grind to a halt? Two people may go through the exact same experience and whereas one continues, on the other hand one can end up in life consumed with grief leading to isolation, alcoholism, drugs or even homelessness.

When my youngest son Shaka died just over three weeks old due to his extreme prematurity I was overwhelmed. I had become a single mother yet again but this time at three months pregnant. I could not believe it (as I said earlier). No goodbye. Twins on the way and living in a council flat with no lift on the second floor. Losing Shaka to neonatal death because he just stopped breathing and no one could resuscitate him was awful words cannot describe the pain. They tried but it was so difficult constantly crying and silently hoping I wouldn't wake up planning who to leave my eldest son to if I died…..the list went on.

But how did I overcome all that?

When I realised I couldn't see a future beyond three days I decided to make everyday a good day doing my best. Taking my eldest son to school, paying my bills, texting others who were ill or worse off, visiting the unit every moment I had because I was too ill to work. I had septicemia at one point and my son spent his first six and a half months of life an inpatient in hospital. I was told he wouldn't survive twenty-four hours. He had numerous operations and I kept a journal. I photographed so many moments, hundreds of photos, I wrote daily, I painted, wrote poetry and I thanked god every moment as I knew there was a lesson. I was already a strong woman as much of my life had been overcoming adversity but this journey (where I gave birth alone and buried my child weeks later wearing white and green) changed something in me. I now help women using my story as I said earlier in this chapter create their life by design on purpose. We need to move on and say goodbye but be thankful for the memories. *So once again why do we need to overcome loss?* It's simple to create a future and live our best life in the present, showing gratitude daily for the good as well as the bad times as these strengthen us. Loved ones are never lost.

That way the past really doesn't determine our future, our life and rewrites our story. Once we grow as spiritual beings having a human experience we really do value everything and can be very detached from it when needed. Sometimes emotionally we can invest a lot in a situation. When I had sick twins and experienced every mother's worst nightmare I could have become reclusive, isolated myself and stayed in the anger of *'why me?'*. I couldn't though because practically and physically I had my other son to look after. I wanted to make this experience as calm as possible for him. I continued with my normal 'mummy duties' and made hospital visits fun by encouraging my eldest to bring his favourite Mr Men books to read to his brother's in intensive care in the neonatal unit in their cots and incubators later on. We bought packed lunch and did everything as normal apart from bringing his brothers home. I was shattered and thought the daily visits would never end. After having one baby die in hospital, every night I left I prayed my surviving twin would be there and I wouldn't get that call again. The one I had before when my heart beat practically stopped beating and I was told I need to come to the hospital urgently because he had gone but they were still working on him thirty minutes later. Again alone rushing to the hospital in a cab alone... how awful! Looking back, I now realise that although a nightmare, I could live in fear my whole life or trust the universe, god and myself that everything would be okay.

It is precisely at times like this that you dig deep and find strength. Rise up and be resilient. That... or crumble under the uncertainty of the journey that is unfolding all of the time. It is in these times something amazing and magical happens within. You either grow or stay stagnated often consumed with the trauma and talking about it to any and everyone who will listen for years. That was me years ago. My closest friend talked of this and tried to bring me out of this for years. God bless her but the journey and long hard lesson was mine I laugh at it now.

Listen to your intuition. The thing that stirs you when you are quiet. Digging deep also means looking for role models. I'm not talking about the famous ones though they have their uses but women you know who may have inspired you especially if they have a story of adversity they have overcome. Never forget that you are a warrior woman and someone who can always find strength. You don't want to be stuck in your story and know that there is some work involved in overcoming issues but remember you and your loved ones family and friends will all benefit more if you are well.

Embracing a circumstance in your life is about embracing yourself and the life you have. *Where you have been? Where you are now?... and where you are going?* Everything happens for a reason so try to stay positive as this is the first step out of the seven in learning how to overcome any adversity.

Quick Tip

Think of a situation (Current or Past), Write it down. What is it you need to do to embrace it fully? From there you can move on to solutions and develop a step by step strategy.

Affirmation

All will be well as long as I accept this situation. Once I accept, I can work on a strategy for overcoming in the best way possible for my highest and greatest good.

Step Two

Motivate Yourself

" I think if you understand that anything is possible, physically write your goals down, and dream big, you can truly see the power of anything you think is possible..."
(Marcia Brock- Thought Leader and Project Director)

MOTIVATE Yourself. Don't spend years waiting for others to Motivate you when everything you seek outside is within. Create your dream life after careful reflection and introspection.

" True Success is a heart captivated by the Love of the one who created us "
(Karen Ross- Administrator for Kensington Temple, London city Church)

So what's so important about daily practices...? Simple really. Daily practices keep you motivated. I don't know what you do but for me most mornings I meditate. I find it relaxing for my soul and it sets me in a positive frame of mind daily. So many people have opinions about that but try it and see if you don't already do this.

I also like to wake up earlier than my children to plan the day, write anything whether it's my journal or gratitude list, drink my Redbush tea and wait as everyone wakes setting my intentions for the day. Some people exercise, jog, walk or find something else they love. No one can tell you what to do but it's a game of trial and error, finding what is manageable and what makes you happy. I would advise you to find a daily routine though. Many times, I hear people saying '*ooh you're so calm*'. It wasn't always like that, but I try to relax, deep breathe, and soak in the energy of my surroundings all day. In the business of life we can become so busy we forget ourselves, our essence, our skills, desires and at times our basic needs. It is at these times we need time to reflect and doing this daily we must. Time alone to reflect even for ten whole minutes a day can help you be able to move mountains. It is a shame there is so much external noise but find ways of being able to reflect by taking a walk., run, bike ride, going away from your usual environment for the day or weekend as these all help. *Do one thing daily to allow you to get that time alone.*

Daily Spiritual practices can help us greatly and keep us motivated. When I talk about spiritual practices I mean for the soul in a non-religious context. Daily practices can set a positive routine or tone to our day and influence us on more levels than we realise. Waking up a bit earlier (as mentioned above), meditation, shower, exercise, journaling and reflecting are all ways you can create a phenomenal high energy and productive routine as well as writing in a journal, gratitude notes in a jar or a highlight on a whiteboard all create a positive focus for the day ahead. Listening to a short twenty minute meditation on YouTube and listening to someone like Les Brown, Dr Wayne Dyer or someone who motivates *you* while you get ready sets you up for a great day so that when the challenges come (and they will) you can ride the waves in a more focused and positive flow of energy and mindset.

Another way to be motivated is by listening to talks, and watching videos. Motivate yourself with positive talk. In a world where people rely on Google rather than books to research, watch and record, it's a great time to take advantage. If you go onto YouTube you will see thousands of talks, channels and music videos so there is no time like the present for listening to motivational talks online. Something I do daily and it is completely free. We have access to the greatest speakers, thinkers and philosophers of all time as well as writers who are alive as well as those who are not. How much more can we ask for in this digital age? Hearing positive talk can inspire you, boost confidence and motivate you when no one or nothing else can. When I started my first business in 2013 it was at a time in my life when I had recently come out of probably one of the worst negative times of my life. My youngest son who was the extremely early surviving twin was seven years old. I had been (and still am) his full-time carer and had been really overwhelmed with life as it was. My eldest son was fifteen and nearly fully independent but it was times of the GCSEs.

He had grown up quite quickly since his brothers were born. I was a lone parent (and still am) although I had the support of my mother who had now taken early retirement, I was wanting to go back to work and some sort of normality. My youngest had been critically ill on and off and my life had been medicalised following trips and down to various hospitals across London under various specialists. He had heart surgery, pneumonia, blood transfusions and various life threatening illnesses. I had even had to resuscitate him numerous times over the first few years of life. I had applied for sixty-seven jobs and only got two interviews for the lowest paid jobs. I wasn't even working for that money when I was sixteen years old and here I was at the age of forty-one with twenty-six years experience and community work in various settings as well as an additional twenty-five plus years of additional education (including my BSc Honours degree) being offered a twenty hour a week job not using any of my skills for less than £7,000 a year. No way! I knew I could do better. So listening to motivational talks online, going to seminars and conferences all helped me to do the often scary unthinkable thing to start my Art, Jewellery and Photograph accessory business. These all helped me to boost my confidence and inspired me to go on a journey of fully embracing the creative 'me'. *Who are you? What do you want in your life? How can you make yourself be more motivated?* (Take at least 10 minutes to think and write down any notes) As with everything else it is a trial and error game that really is worth playing!

Uplifting/ inspiring books for the Soul boost confidence so it's important to read something positive every day even if a few quotes and especially on waking. Reading daily and although it's doesn't have to be a whole book, it is a fantastic way to learn, grow and be inspired. There is so much to learn and we can never know it all. I am saddened when people say they have nothing else to learn. We can never stop learning and as someone labelled by others as an eternal scholar we really never can. So it's safe to say reading can uplift your spirits, boost confidence and possibly improve your self-esteem. *What are you currently reading?* Of course it pays to be choosy about what it is you are reading. I used to love reading the newspapers every day but if you stand back and pay attention, you realise that no matter how positive you are reading the mainstream media is very disheartening, worrying and at best more negative than your general day-to-day thinking. I personally stopped reading newspapers and watching the news a few years ago. I now read the news when I feel like it on the internet, usually choosing to focus on more positive media, books and News stories.

So what else can you do to motivate yourself? Many people like to create a Vision board. As well as our daily practices, a fantastic way to stay continually motivated is to have a visual reminder we can physically look at. People have their own views as to how to create one and there are many ways but the overall essence is to think about your big dreams and goals, cut-out pictures, words and write words sticking them on to your paper or board. This is something I do with clients in module two as it is important to know where you are heading. We all have dreams. **Do you know what your dreams are?** *Or are you stuck in the busyness of fulfilling roles and carrying out duties?* Visually seeing your dreams allows your brain to think it possible. The old adage seeing is believing rings true and does work. I always have a vision board and am teaching my twelve-year old son to do the same. My eldest son is somewhat reluctant because he prefers to use his logical brain and rely on the picture he paints inside, but he's twenty and has his own way. I personally have used vision boards on and off over the last twenty years having years of gaps but since using consistently for the last five years, I seem to be achieving much more. Vision boards also allow you to think about what you want. You would be surprised by the amount of women I have spoken to who are not even sure what their dreams are beyond family, children or work. I know because although I always had dreams, I can remember being asked what I did for fun by a male friend maybe twelve years ago and I was stumped. I had gone from having fun with friends numerous times a week to moving out of London to Birmingham for a year, no family support, no friends, a fiance who was out more hours than in severe loneliness to top it all off as well as a new baby (my first) in a place where I spent all day house cleaning and watching daytime TV. When I moved back to London when our relationship ended (when my son was six months old) the shame, guilt for leaving a relationship that became unhealthy was too much so i decided to stay in most of the time when not working at my old job was a way of life. I was easier. *So why tell you all this?*

One reason..... At that time I can honestly say I had no dreams at least not ones I saw or remember. I was devastated being a new mum and at the time felt so shameful now being a single mum (the one stereotype I never wanted to be). Embarrassment when people asked why I wasn't married by now and why I had returned to London when I so adamantly left the year before five or six months pregnant to start a new life in Birmingham. I was in survival (day-to-day) mode trying to make a life unsure of where I was going. *Have you been in that place?* Sometimes it serves a purpose, other times it holds you back. It took me years to also find out that most successful entrepreneurs and people have a vision board. This is as important as your daily diary or planner especially if you have a family. You may even need a separate Family goals vision board, Couples one and Your own individual one. Either way it's important to note your dreams down to stop them floating around in your head or being forgotten at worst.

Why set goals? What's the reason and purpose? Because goals precede dreams. We have all heard the saying a dream without a goal is a wish. Well I would go one step further and say and a 'goal without a vision is worthless'. ***How many times have you dreamt about doing something and become distracted with*** *life.?* It's so easy. We are not taught in schools to have the entrepreneurial mind. Whether business owners or not, this mindset means we are more often open to opportunities and big dreams. Setting goals helps us to gain clarity and can allow us to see a pathway we may never have thought of. The time I mentioned before when I applied for sixty-seven jobs made me realise that with all of my experience and training maybe I should think about my vision and goals rather than just a job. I had no vision board but writing notes I realised that I definitely didn't want to work for anyone else again so I started to create a vision. I I realised small steps work best and I went about designing my vision for a better life. Now is the time to create yours. *What kind of life do you want to create?* Time to pause and have a think! Write down the experiences, travel, activities, career and family life you want to have.

On our journey to stay motivated (and it is a journey), reflection on the good as well as bad times are important. We are the sum of all our parts. Your challenges create your strengths. When people used to say this to me years ago my first response was *yeah right* they're probably the lucky ones. I always knew about mindset and although I was a firm believer, I wasn't as positive as I had initially thought. I would look back on my challenges as flaws and weaknesses as if I was broken and everyone else has absolutely perfect. That was not the case. When I got to the age of thirty-four I couldn't have been more disappointed with myself for ending up pregnant with twins after a five month romance and being left to it by the father. Fast forward to having the twins at twenty-three weeks, losing my youngest Shaka at twenty three days old and having my eldest twin an inpatient for six and a half months. Starting off in intensive neonatal care for the first four months, Special care and then promoted to Paediatrics.....you get the picture. When I thought I had bad times before, that was nothing like this. I'm not saying you need to have experienced anything as traumatic but what I will say is *don't underestimate the strengths your challenges create*. I truly believe that everything happens for a reason. Now I look back on the many experiences over the years and I'm grateful for everyone who has ever helped, as well as hurt me. Those who supported as well as pulled me down. Those who elevated as well as dismantle me and those who were so happy for me when others were spitefully not. *Is this something you believe?* **Make a list of some of your hardest challenges and the lessons learnt or the positive that came out eventually**. If you can't think of them don't worry your journey/ learning with that challenge is still ongoing. This, along with other ways will encourage you to overcome challenges. Life is about learning. All our experiences, childhood stories, background, work and health stories make us all unique. You know this already though but *do you really appreciate you? Everything you have been through! Every trauma! Every blessing! And everything in between.!*

That leads me quite nicely into what self-compassion is and how we can show it. A very debatable subject but the harsh reality is self love proceeds all love. A huge statement I know but it is profound for a reason. A concept I personally never really fully embraced until I reached my late thirties. I had grown up watching my wonderful and kind hearted selfless mother doing everything for everyone else always putting herself last so I modelled much of my own behaviour on that. How could I not? We learn by example. So as the years passed and I saw others caring for themselves first and showing self-compassion I thought they were highly selfish. I had gone into voluntary work at the tender age of fifteen convinced I needed to save the world because my childhood experiences influenced me to think most people were wicked, selfish, uncaring and downright evil at times. We lived in a house where domestic violence was present and the trauma for about seven years apparently made me distrust people. I knew my mum was a wonderful human being but her lack of self love, coupled with her mother's premature death and estrangement from her rest of her family certainly never helped her with her own self-esteem and confidence. *So why bother share all this....?* Simple really so you can gather a picture of what I'm talking about and map a similar time/ story in your own life that may resonate with you. One of the first acts of self-compassion is to forgive yourself. I don't mean think *yeah I forgive myself.* I mean actually say it out loud. There are some wonderful ways in which to do this type of work and yes it is paramount in motivating yourself though not what we have been taught to do again. The ancient Hawaiian Forgiveness ritual Ho'oponopono is the key and after practicing this for about thirty days straight it opened up things in me I had forgotten, couldn't remember and really had no idea I was holding onto. Nothing strips you quite so bare as holding a mirror up, looking at yourself and saying

"I love you", **"I'm sorry"** (followed by whatever it is you are sorry for) **"Please forgive me"** and **"Thank you"**. Of course, like anything I suggest in this book find your own way and please above all else listen to your own intuition. Self-care is another important aspect of self-compassion. They say others treat you how you treat yourself so get into the habit of caring for yourself. A day doing something adventurous, having a long bath, appointment at the hairdressers whatever it is that gives you the time to think about *you* and *you only*. Self-compassion can also be us being authentic standing in our truth. If we are asked to do something and we really don't want want to do it not only can we grow resentful, but we can also compromise our self our beliefs and at worst our values. These are the underpinning qualities of our authenticity therefore learning to say 'No' is one of the most important skills in life. ***How do you show Self Compassion..?***

In order to keep motivated it's also important to look at our community. They say we are the sum of our closest friends. This is so true. No matter how much we may personally try to deny this it is worth thinking about. Having a support network is paramount and trying to keep that with positive people can make all the difference. Whilst being on this journey we call life, it is important to be surrounded by people who can encourage, champion, help us focus and hold us accountable. My personal development journey started as a child. Asking questions, reading, trying to understand people, behaviour, cultures, violence and overall psychology. Looking at myself was more focused in my late teens then early twenties. I can honestly say though that due to my programs and upbringing (especially as a scared person generally), I was hugely resistant to change. Ask my closest friend and she could tell you a thing or two. My constant saying even until my thirties was *'I'm frightened'*. She coached me through so much and tried to get me to be as fearless as she was taking opportunities often first then working it out after. I, on the other hand worked the other way around seeing it possible then saying yes. During our now thirty years of friendship I'm eternally grateful for every conversation, every tear, every telling off and every push above and beyond my comfort zone. My other closest friend supported me in a very different way nurturing my abilities talents and dreams. ***What kind of network have you got?*** Have a think about it. I believe we have a number of networks but see what resonates best with you. Currently as I become more involved in my business my main support network is primarily other business owners, predominantly women. I still have many nearest and dearest friends, family and fun friends who I don't talk any business or personal development with. Having a sense of community is key as well as a sense of belonging too. Don't underestimate this. The saying no man is an island is true. I used to be more of a loner at times due to serious trust issues. At times I would be so insular and literally shut off from the world. It was hard for others around me who questioned depression but as I was always highly functioning and did the Mummy duties etc as a lone parent as well I never sought medical advice. I was a warrior. A survivor. With a community you have a shared commonality so don't underestimate the power of that. Think about the ways in which your community motivates and empowers you and if it is negative come to some decision as to how you will handle that as it will affect you negatively in the long run.

Surrounding yourself with inspiring events such as conferences, seminars, talks and workshops is another way to motivate yourself when going through serious challenges. The day-to-day of life can sometimes be overwhelming with the ebb and flow so being surrounded with like-minded people inspires and uplifts you as well as increases your self-esteem. There have been times especially when I really started coming into myself in my mid thirties that I felt I didn't belong anywhere anymore. I needed more than I was getting. I was caring full-time for my youngest who was sick and life consisted of way too many hospital appointments, medication, worries about oxygen and breathing as he was still dependent and a huge fear of loss. I should have been happy to have my baby home but I was so preoccupied with sudden death secretly which came from the fact that my youngest son stopped breathing suddenly and couldn't be resuscitated. The autopsy had been inconclusive. I had already had to bury one child and agree to pay a bit extra in case they needed to reopen the grave to bury the surviving twin and what an awful decision that was to make alone, I wouldn't want to wish that on anyone. The reason I say this is because even through some of our darkest hours, seminars around mindset, the power of your thoughts and living your best life gave me hope. Many were online at that particular time and when I did go to the live events, it was at times life-changing. Something in me had changed. I couldn't explain it and it took a few years to come to fruition but my old ways of thinking had changed. My priorities had moved and I was floating into new territory. Due to the intense twenty-four hour caring I was doing that took my mind off the cocoon stage I was going through before becoming the butterfly and I happily plotted along for another few years. Then the time came time to indulge in new adventures. New Adventures create new outlooks. *What new adventures could you do with creating?* It's always good to take a life inventory. New experiences have a way of growing us. When we look for motivation many of us still look externally to others to motivate us. That works to a degree but the main way of staying motivated is to motivate yourself. In regard to new adventures picture something you have been thinking about doing and finally pluck up the courage to do it. It could be going for a dinner alone, speaking in public or more extreme like a bungee jump. *What happens before, during and after doing it? How did you feel?* During this time whatever the 'thing' is, it teaches us more about ourselves. We sometimes find a courage and focus we never knew we had. In 2000 when my first son was only two years old I decided to do something very significant and take a lone trip to Egypt for fifteen days. I had thought about this for years from a child as energetically I had always felt a connection beyond my understanding to Africa especially (Ancient Kemit also known as) Egypt. I had dreamt about this ancient place for years and believe I was a sage many lifetimes ago (though that is another book in itself). I had split with my fiance then and was still in the midst of devastation, turmoil and not knowing where I was going to go from there. Childcare would be an issue. I had never left my son longer than a day. My mum was working as well as his father who lived in Birmingham and all I had was the fifty pounds for a deposit for a group tour with complete strangers and a part-time job where I had to put whatever I had weekly to pay for both the tour and trip. With all logistics sorted I departed early December and had a life-changing experience. Adventures teach us things we would never imagine and a side of us only needed to develop at that time. It also motivated me to travel and know that if I waited until I had all of the money I would never have went. This trip motivated me to take more risks and even to climb Mount Sinai which I had never done before. In fact, I had never climbed a mountain in my life so think about what new adventures you can have to find hidden parts of you, you never knew existed. I chose to travel. You can choose something else. Travel can be a useful tool to motivate us. Experiencing various cultures teaches us an appreciation by seeing the differences in our culture. We also learn new things and will at some point during the trip increase our compassion as well as gratitude for what we have. There is nothing like seeing reminders up close and personal. Something else I personally found very rewarding over the years for motivating myself is to help others. Helping others makes you look at yourself and your life differently often increasing appreciation and can also be a form of therapy. Volunteering is a great way to help serve others and increases selflessness. We can also learn new skills and be surrounded by new people. Working for others (especially unpaid) motivates us on all levels increasing confidence and courage. I have volunteered in many fields of the community over the last thirty years and learnt so much. It has motivated me to be grateful and has been hugely rewarding. Starting in Adventure playgrounds with 5- 16 year olds, onto Prison visitor for lifers whose family had disowned them due to their crimes, working with people with HIV/ AIDS in health promotion, Arts ambassador, on a magazine panel for Bliss the premature baby charity to name but a few. All of these experiences enriched my life and have played a significant factor in who I am today. ***What adventures will you take starting today to motivate yourself.?***

Quick Tip

Find ways to motivate yourself daily (i.e. Listening to talks, audio, reading books, watching videos, quiet time, meditation) and create a manageable daily routine. Start small until you have the desired plan. A ten minute routine may be the most you can manage at present so get into doing that regularly before you increase the time.

Affirmation

I AM going to rise up and live my life on purpose regardless of my circumstances. Only I can motivate myself. Everything I need is within me. I declare it and So it is!

Step Three

Power over your Life

" You have the Power to get through anything. Your talent, intuition, personal qualities and values are YOUR SuperPowers. Believe in them "

(Serena Nalty-Coombs- Project Management Consultant, Mentor, Entrepreneur)

POWER over *your* Life. You are in the driving seat regardless of your Story and Experiences. You do not have to be a Victim of your Circumstances, be Soul Conscious Creators.

" There is no point in having a mind if you aren't free to Change it "

(Ola Agbaimoni- Founder of the 7 Momentous Moments Coaching process & Founder and Former CEO of Eelan Media, Interfaith Minister and Head of Programme delivery (London) at NHS England)

So beautiful….. you have made it this far in the book and still reading, so I assume you are ready to take back the power over your life….! Well it really isn't as hard as we may think. We are not the sum of our circumstances. S*** happens as the saying goes and you have to deal with it. *What do you do when things go wrong or bad? Do you know your patterns?* When I became a single parent with my first child when he was six months old I really understood the expression life throwing you curveballs. I remember feeling like such a failure and a victim. I had been the one to move back to London. He wasn't willing to move. I was also the one a number of weeks later left holding the baby (my first child). I looked like a victim and sure as hell felt like one, but over a number of years later realised I wasn't. I wasn't a victim. I was a woman in (to me) the worst life-changing situation I could have been in. I was a single mother which I found difficult to come to terms with and only because my fiance had kept going on about having children especially a girl. Here I was, someone who wanted to travel extensively and so didn't envisage children until my mid thirties if at all. I was now with a son who was fatherless and being judged by every individual who frowned when they realised I was a lone parent. Okay I was twenty-six but still, a black woman from Hackney (one of the poorest boroughs in London then) constantly told we were disadvantaged inner-city children now an adult fulfilling the stereotype. It took a long time (and I mean years) to realise that you cannot be held accountable for other people's actions and it's not always your fault. A relationship breakdown is often down to both parties in some form or another.

I was now a single mother yes, but I was also Hyacinth and she was an avid community worker, creative, artist, writer, poet. She was also constantly upgrading her training, life goals and ambitions although still not at her fullest potential. This was ultimately a time to learn and grow.

So then I'll ask the question, **How or why are you feeling stuck?** Many of you may be feeling powerless. Well let's break that down a bit. *Why are you feeling powerless?* In Absolutely every situation we have choices. We can give up and say *'there's nothing I can do about it'* or we can look at it as an outsider and decide regardless, we are not going to allow this to define our future. Feeling powerless is a natural occurrence but *being in a state of powerlessness long-term is a choice.* One of the most common reasons for staying stuck is that sometimes we are unable to move on and forgive. Forgiveness is a word people can sometimes be afraid of but really shouldn't be. It is the only way to overcome whatever it is you feel or know the person has done to you. It's something I personally found extremely difficult as my core values are honesty, integrity and justice. I came across a fantastic hawaiian practice of reconciliation and forgiveness called the Ho'oponopono as mentioned earlier. A friend of mine reminded me of it a few years after I'd first heard of it and done what we sometimes do, got busy and forget about it. You can use it with others or for self forgiveness. For many others including myself (for years) they may be stuck due to the replaying of the story. Although I never became stuck in my story long enough to suffer diagnosed depression, I was nonetheless believing that my limitations were mostly due to my story. Without realising it, I was constantly talking about the past but living in the present. *Are you replaying the story? How much time do you spend talking about the past and giving the power to others?* We must not let our past define our future. My signature quote is simple, no gimmicks or play with words, just my thoughts as a poet and writer who meditates and often gets messages.....

"We don't have to be Victims of our circumstances, We can be Soul Conscious Creators of our Future".

Having power over your life also means thinking about (at the very basic level) how you manage your emotions. In stressful situations it's useful at times to take a minute or two out to breathe and pause. That way we reduce the power others have by reducing becoming emotionally charged and less likely to act on impulse which we can do at times. Staying calm during a challenging situation can be such a godsend. It can stop you overreacting, making a situation worse and reduce helplessness. Counting and re-centering can be beneficial. *What ways do you stay calm when someone pushes your buttons?* When my eldest son was very trying at about the age of six and seven I used to count to refocus before responding to whatever he had done most of the time. I was working on reducing shouting which is something I personally dislike doing. It did work well at times especially if I had become angry and had to diffuse that. Often my annoyance would be triggered by past events where I felt disrespected and were almost like reminders being repeated. ***Do you know when is a good time to count and re-centre, or pause and breathe?*** It's something we all must all be aware of if we want to be empowered. We control our emotions no one else. So try not to get wrapped up in your feelings. Our feelings are *our* perspective and as we know put a group of people at the scene of the same situation and you'll get as many variations on what occurred as there are people. I'm not saying don't acknowledge you are angry or hurt, but rather than act, decide to do something peaceful and affirming at the time. Sometimes taking back your power can be something as simple as saying nothing, reducing contact with negative people, or waiting to reply to that email that really annoyed you to more extreme, walking away from a hostile/ volatile situation rather than arguing until the bitter. Either way who has control now?

In order to take back power over your life, that also includes family, friends and work. Family should be a joy and not a burden so think about setting up routines and structure if you don't already have them. It can make life easier by saving time and reduces your need to constantly have to coordinate this and helps everyone in the long run. It teaches life skills not taught in schools apart from the usual punctuality and lesson structure. Life however is more complicated however and can lead to children and partner's becoming more independent. ***How do you manage***

your family life? *Take an honest look.* I hear many women complaining about the children but when looking deeper there is sometimes little structure or routines. We all need structure to feel secure in what we do and life in general, children are not exempt. That leads me quite nicely onto the subject of delegating tasks. I have two sons and when my eldest was about five or six I started to introduce him to doing more regular chores. Only small at that time, tidying his room, hanging up his boxer shorts on the washing line and putting them away when dry. Bringing his plate etc to the kitchen when finished. It caused so many discussions and disagreements. He already had a bedtime routine as a baby and would be in bed by 6.30pm much to the annoyance of others who all felt I was being too harsh. My thinking was that as a single mother I was not going to make him solely dependent on me so he would have to participate and learn about responsibility early. Now he's twenty years old I can see the benefits because he is highly independent and since the age of eighteen has been financially independent of me though still at home. That is a joy and pleasure to see.

Another way I personally take back power over my life is to go away regularly. Days out but weekends away a few times a year without children too. It took me years to do this, but I started to realise that because I have a hectic fast-paced life, going away leaving all the noise behind, is something I personally need to stay mentally well. London can be a noisy place and is a built-up area with new builds practically everywhere. Some people won't need to physically leave their environment, but I definitely do. It's been my god send but I'm lucky to have an amazing mother who helps me so much I personally wouldn't have been able to achieve much without her practical support with both of my sons.

So what is the best way to take back power over your work?
Well one way is to do something you enjoy. You don't have to kill yourself in work you hate anymore. We have been conditioned to think this but the courageous break free from this mentality and end up pursuing their dreams. Some of you will be working for others, moving jobs or setting up their own businesses. Research shows that staying in any work you hate eventually affects your health physically and mentally negatively. This ultimately corresponds with the rise in illnesses overall. I believe that much of what we experience is environmental. With statistics quoted from MIND the Mental Health charity that one in four people will suffer mental health problems in the UK let alone the world figures. So think about this.....*are you happy with your work? If so, there's absolutely nothing you have to do but if not, sit down and do a skills audit?* **What are you good at? Strengths? What do you need to improve? What really gets you out of your bed in the morning.?** Why not take a test such as a D.I.S.C Profile or The Vitality Test (Five Institute) or a Numerology Natal chart to get a clearer understanding of yourself. You really will be surprised with the findings. You will have a better understanding of yourself

and more than just what you and others think. With this information you can get a clearer understanding of yourself and then look into what your dreams and aspirations are from a different perspective. After I had my second son twelve years ago. I had years as his full-time carer until school age and when he started school I still had a high number of hospital appointments. I was still doing volunteering work but choosing my hours and knew I wanted to get back into paid work. I was never a nine to fiver, but all I could see was poorly paid, unskilled jobs as the alternative for a lone parent looking for something to fit within the school run. I was even told by the jobcentre at the time, to get a cleaning job although I have my BSc honours degree in Social Policy with Criminal Justice, various Diplomas, Certificates and twenty-something years Community work experience as well as twenty-years post school education and training. Needless to say I thought *no way am I going to settle for this* and found out about becoming self-employed. My youngest was six then and still undiagnosed with the cognitive difficulties and Special Educational Needs he has. *Now I do the work I love so Thank You Universe for not allowing me to find that job.* You can do the same.!

The next phase is to make your dreams a reality. **But why make your dreams a reality at all?** Many people don't. One of my favourite speakers Les Brown has so many stories and anecdotes about this. I think the most important reason is because we all deserve happiness. When we live our dreams, we are much happier. Everybody's dreams are as personal and unique as our of fingerprints are. My dream has always been to travel and work within communities ever since I was a child. I gave up the *one job* idea and laugh when people still say *what do you do? I'm confused.* Apparently we should be known for one love or one thing only but when you enter the world of business you realise people like us are called Entrepreneurs, Innovators, Visionaries and Creatives. Living life on your terms is such a wonderful thing. When you are doing what you love it feels as if you are not working at all. You hear so many people saying it but it really is true. Just think back to the times you have been so immersed in something, enjoying it and seen hours fly by. Isn't it such a wonderful feeling? **So what dreams do you want to make into a reality?** *Why don't you take 10 minutes right now and write it down, braindump.* **If money or time was not a barrier, what dreams do you have?** Your dreams can only manifest from you so stop trying to live the dreams others have for you. They can be limiting or completely unaligned to you. A final thought in regard to making your dreams a reality is that, your dreams/ your purpose maybe to serve others and if you don't manifest the dream fully many people won't benefit from being touched by you. For many years my calling has been to empower others but the last three years especially women. I was talking my own self out of it. Telling myself and others that I'd be just another female empowerment coach in an oversaturated market. Why bother? It took some of my nearest and dearest to convince me to go for it regardless.

I soon realised that the broken and hidden parts of me were my difference. Nothing like lived experience in order to mentor others successfully. Also as the Empower 7 programme came to me through meditation, dreams, visions, etc how could I justify keeping it to myself? My unique selling point is experience and the way it was created as well as Intuitive coaching/ mentoring. So service has been a theme for me for the last thirty years, this is just a continuation!

That moves me quite nicely into how you can make a difference. Many people are busy caught up in life and the mundane routine of being in a full time job. A large number don't like working, getting home late, being shattered and either breaking even with the bank account or constantly in overdraft. There comes a time when we need to reflect on life. When we think we can't make a difference often we do and can. When I became a lone parent for the second time so many people suggested I give up all of the voluntary jobs I was doing. I didn't. I was doing three so cut down to two but I was still able to impact and change others lives for the better. Reflecting on life is a fantastic thing to do as we can grow but staying stuck as a victim is so unhelpful both to yourself and others. Don't be a victim. It serves no one. I know there are people who may say to you 'that's alright for you to say but...', honestly many of us have stories. I could quite easily sit down and replay major life incidents and justify being a victim. I did for a while but long after you have been hurt, embarrassed and abused the other person has forgotten so why give them the pleasure of ruining your life? why? Life is *for* you *not* against you! Mindset makes all the difference. ***What things are keeping you from making the difference? What do you need to do? What do you need to change?*** *Stop looking outside and look within because all you can really Change Is You!*

In order to use all experiences in our lives positively, there are a number of things we can do. One of the most important but probably hardest is to depersonalise it. Our experiences when we are hurt are very emotional. We try to seek answers, may reel in anger about what they did to us, replay the scenario and tell everybody about it. All of these practices are not very useful to us. All they do is reinforce the personal nature of what happened to us and our perception according to our own previous experiences. When you look at a situation from an objective perspective it is less personal. For example, single parenting I internalised so much feeling completely ashamed that here I am with two children and two absent fathers though differing scenarios. Others judge but I judged much harder. *How could an otherwise sensible woman end up here?* First time round myself and eldest son's dad were together just over five years and engaged before it all fell apart. Second time here I was again, this time pregnant by a man nine years my junior whom I'd had a five month relationship with. It was only when I told him he decided to walk away, threatened my pregnancy and harassed me because he couldn't cope with being a dad. It was nothing to do with me in that sense but was his problem. It was only then I decided to make the best of a bad situation though over the first three years he was to flit in and out of my son's life until finally I had to stop contact for safety concerns. *What situations personally can you turn that negative into a positive.?* *Take a moment to think*!

Another way of overcoming negative experiences is to look on the bright side. I know everyone hears this and it can appear cliche but when you're going through a serious challenge it can be hard to implement. I certainly found this extremely difficult for years. The thing is when you are going through difficulties the best way to stay focused on the positive, is to make sure you are trying to balance the scales. I now have a routine that works well for me. If things are tough, I make sure in between these I do things I love, things that make me happy and my love is to create. Create poems to release the feelings, create something artistic maybe jewellery, art, paint and take photos in nature during a visit to place of interest. I rarely call someone to discuss and replay the situation anymore as this was really draining for me and only put me into quite a negative spiral and frame of mind calling in more negativity. *What positive things can you do? Or do you do already?* *Make a list when you can see for yourself.*

So with all this I'm assuming you have come across gratitude work! If not, it's exactly what it says on the tin. Regardless of my experiences I am thankful for…..(followed by the sentence with

46

whatever you are grateful for). Everyday write down at least three things you are grateful for. Lately mine has included, for waking up today in my right mind, for the many little blessings I receive daily but may be too busy to see too. It makes me more mindful. I like to put mine in a gratitude jar and reminds you that no matter how bad things get you can always get through it. That alone helps to see that this negative experience is here to teach you something for the better and regardless of my experiences I am thankful!

So Why is self esteem so important? For a number of reasons. One being that self-esteem helps us to take changes, grab opportunities and help us step closer to fulfilling our dreams or purpose. Low self-esteem can often mean we are scared to take chances and can leave many of us scared to try in the first place. That's the reason why building on it as individuals is important. So many people leave this world not living their life on purpose, by design and definitely without passion. Doing things that help you take back your power are empowering in themselves. Self-esteem is important when it comes to setting boundaries and is vital for self care. Without healthy boundaries life can get very complicated and excessively tiring. Being able to say no, show others what you will and will not accept and put down stop signs all help you to build your own self esteem. A prime example is that when we are tired and do something we should have said no to. Then not only do we regret it and resent it (whatever that is), but we also feel worse about ourselves and incompetent about then speaking our truth then reinforces feelings of inadequacy, feeling pathetic and weak. The age old adage then has to be *if you don't love you then who will?* Best take this in for a moment! Breathe and really dwell on that for a minute....**How is your Self esteem feeling? Are you aware of it? Do you know how to increase it if needed?**

Just as self esteem is important, so is confidence and the ways in which we can build our own. I personally use daily affirmations and have found them extremely useful over the years. I used to use other people's ones but now use my own mostly which I create after meditation every few months. This is something I do with clients in the Motivation module. Daily affirmations help to keep you focused and reinforce positive ways of thinking. Many people find them useful. ***Are there any sayings or positive sentences or affirmations you use already? Are there some you want to create?*** Being around positive people also helps build confidence. Whether in the world of work or just in your personal life, try and surround yourself with people who will encourage you to be your best all of the time. It's very disheartening being with people who are negative and trying to build your self esteem at the same time. It's like trying to walk up a hill on roller skates. You probably can do it but it will take so much longer unnecessarily. Keeping a note of our achievements is another fantastic way of building our confidence. If you achieve something you are proud of tell your

48

nearest and dearest or friends. Celebrating a job well done, drinks with friends reinforces the achievement. It's also a good way especially for a couple of friends and acquaintances to really build confidence and support for each other.

Power over your life includes learning how to manage stress. Stress is one of the biggest killers in the UK and biggest causes of depression, anxiety, mental health problems, high blood pressure list goes on. Looking at situations individually really does help to reduce the impact it has on you. For example something challenging happens and you say either *this is the situation what are the possible solutions?* rather than *this has happened to me again/ bad things always happen/ I've got bad luck only few weeks ago….. and it's because and nothing ever goes right.* Can you see the difference now? **Recognise yourself there anywhere?** I was always the one who clumped every bad thing together to find out later on that for my own peace of mind I needed to separate them. Being mindful daily is a great way of managing stress. By this I don't mean the art of being in awe (as some believe mindfulness to be) but more about noticing what you think, how this makes you feel and your reactions. Some things in the past that would have really annoyed me or upset me now don't. I still don't like it but instead I have chosen to not to allow it to have the same impact. Sure, there were times things do but overall I choose not to get annoyed and take it on. There are more important things to do, see and achieve rather than wasting energy sweating the small stuff.

Some stress is good but as we know too much stress causes damage. Take time out!! *repeat*.....Take time out of your normal routine!! At the most basic a walk, long bath, visiting friends or on the other end of the spectrum is to leave your town, city, for the day or a few days. I can only suggest. We all have such varying ideas and desires about what fun is for us though. Personally, I love to be able to go somewhere to do some landscape photography or disappear for two or three days to a hotel outside of London where I'm not Mum, I don't have to cook or wash up. A complete break from my business too and just enjoy precious time with loved ones. ***What do you like to do?*** *Make a list of all the fun things you love to do or want to try at least once and find a way of scheduling that into your diary. Take time out too either a day or a certain amount of days per month.*

In addition to taking time out, is to practice a life of Self love. Contrary to popular belief, self love is not selfish. Self love and self care is extremely important in taking back power. Saying no occasionally to those endless request for help or assistance when you really don't have the energy works. I used to say yes to practically everything and began resenting it when I realised I was the only one willing to sacrifice my peace of mind, time and become burnt out. On reflection I now realise I was not practicing any self love and definitely not valuing myself, my worth, my family and most importantly my time. As a business owner you realise that your time is priceless and at worst worth more than unlimited free yeses. Time for another honest inventory of what you do for your self care. *How do you practise Self Love?* All of these things matter and make a difference. Journaling daily can help to look at self care, worries, achievements and anything else you feel compelled to write about. Many people find it a welcome release from the hustle and bustle and it's something I have been doing for many years as well as recommend clients to do. A great writer I know called Jackie Holder has a book called *49 Ways to Write yourself Well* and goes into more detail about the mental health benefits of journaling. Something I recommend you read more about. Why not buy yourself a wonderful new special book and use that as your journal? It's always better to get into a daily routine but if that is difficult then a few times a week is better to begin with. When you find your routines it will come more naturally and you will find your own rhythm. We can't talk about self love without mentioning the most amazing Hawaiian practice of forgiveness and reconciliation the Ho'oponopono which was mentioned before but for Self. Using the four simple phrases for self love ideally practice in front of a mirror 'I love you', 'please forgive me', 'thank you', 'sorry' . So simple but powerful. It can be used to think of situations involving others (as mentioned previously) or yourself and has had me in floods of tears. Think about a situation and recite the words. Let the healing feeling arise and go with whatever feelings occur. I personally have found this especially useful for situations when you can't get closure from someone who has hurt you deeply for a variety of reasons and you may not ever see them physically again or they may just choose to avoid any further interaction with you. In regard to taking back your power with self love try and focus the forgiveness and situations more on yourself though if possible. Whatever happens in your life and whatever you have done to yourself for whatever reason at that time, you cannot carry the burden of that forever.

Quick Tip

How will you take back Power? Now is the time to plan your life and goals. Use your intuition with your power. Name three situations you feel unresloved in and do the method. How do you feel now?

Affirmation

I AM always in control of my life because I always have choices. I will take back my power. Happiness is my birthright!

Step Four
Overcoming Adversity

" Flood your mind with Positivity and use negative situations to FUEL YOURSELF FORWARD. Don't wait for that light at the end of the tunnel because if you look hard enough you will be able to find light even on the darkest day "
(Veena V- YouTube Coach/ Mentor and Founder of Mum To Millionaire)

OVERCOME ADVERSITY because living in Past causes you to feel Stuck in your Life, Unhappy, Depressed and Anxious. You have been through it Physically now it's time to move through it mentally in a supportive way.

Everything teaches us something so it's really important to accept what has happened in order to move on. The saying the truth shall set you free is accurate. Sometimes in painful situations we can bury our head in the sand and hope it all goes away but there is nothing like facing the truth and dealing with it head on. When we don't, we continue to live in a cycle of the past and I personally believe that this is one of the reasons why mental illnesses/ challenges such as depression are on the increase. With statistics in the UK at an all time high (one in three) people are suffering from anxiety and depression. When I look back at my life and that of others, the only difference I see is how we view our adversities and whether we continue to be stuck in our past. I'm not saying there wasn't times but long-term I really didn't stay there. I'd get quite angry and say to myself and a good friend that person didn't even have half of the things happen to them that I did but are stuck there why? At times I honestly at times didn't have much sympathy either. Now I really do understand her comment when she said that it's all relative and even more since being surrounded by many who practice Mindset Mastery. I realise what a blessing it is to look at a situation differently. When challenges occur and life throws you curveballs moving on and seeing the lesson to learn all help with a way forward. When I became a single mother for the second time nothing could have prepared me for the greatest lessons I was about to learn over the next few years and continually up to now. Resilience I could never have imagined, a passion and assertiveness I never had before and of course endurance and lessons in intuition. When you have to resuscitate your child and exist on two hours sleep with up to sixteen different medications to administer in differing doses, along with weaning off 24 hr Oxygen dependency (with professionals from my local hospital who regularly didn't turn up for home visits) without an organised plan, you have nothing but intuition and faith. Myself, my intuition, a few trusted medical friends and the medical knowledge I had acquired along the way all helped with that.

So how do you accept what's happened and move on...?
Pause and have a think. I could quite easily have said look at me... One child.. Twins... One has died now I'm caring at the most intense, frightening level with no one home to comfort me, or give me a five minute break. I didn't give up. I pushed through the many times I was felt like giving up. You can do that too regardless of whatever it is you are going through.

In order to overcome adversity, self reflection and journaling are so important. Reflecting on past challenges not only gives us insights, it also allows us to see the good, the bad and the ugly in its fullest most raw state. Thinking about a situation is completely different to writing about and recalling it. Journaling can also be used to celebrate achievements as well as other written information. Sometimes we take our achievements for granted but seeing them written down gives us more of a sense of accomplishment. It not only reinforces the achievement, but it also encourages us to achieve more by slaying those dreams. Self reflection and journaling also reduce negative self talk. I remember being in a constant state of negativity and thinking as well as believing all of my internal negative critical chatter. I was never *good enough*. Nothing I did was ever good enough although many said I did a fantastic job I personally didn't believe it. **Do you do that? do you talk yourself out of things? Do you chastise yourself when you would never dream to do that to others?** *Time to take an honest inventory.*

So why do we need to embrace our life up until now to overcome our story? Well a number of reasons really. *Our past is just that! It's not our future!* In order to overcome adversities we need to be accepting and fulfilled. By that I mean, realise that *whatever we did* at the time was our best with the state of mind we were in. Reflecting means looking at what we learned, what we did well, what we can improve on and then move onto the acceptance part. Without fully accepting a serious challenge or problem we cannot move onto overcoming it. *Have you ever met anyone who is still stuck in talking about situations that happened years ago but still not accepted it?* They weren't honest in the part they played and honesty is just as important in overcoming. **What haven't you been honest with yourself about that has caused you harm or taking you much longer to overcome as a result?** *We all have them and no one is exempt!*

Healing from the past opens possibilities for a happier future. How we heal from our adversities determines the possibilities we create and how open we are to them. It's so important to be objective in all situations. I know it's easy to say because I remember being so emotionally charged at times with a constant negative cloud hanging over me, but it's the *only* way to overcome. View it like a maths problem. *What do we do?* Usually there is a formula to solve a problem. The idea is no matter how hard the equation we are aiming to find the answer and as we know there are a number of routes to find the correct answer. Life can be viewed the same. Rather than get caught up in the 'this is too hard' scenario or talk about it for days, weeks or years, take action and say 'let me try this' and 'if it doesn't work, let me try that'. Staying positive is the key. You've heard the saying nothing lasts forever and we never get more than we can bear. There is light at the end of the tunnel (and some tunnels are longer than others). After all of that we can think about what lessons we have learned and as many of us know we always seem to grow through adversity. Believe it or not, our default is not to break down though as we know sometimes it is needed in order for some of us to rebuild. Think about it. *What have you learned? In some of your most difficult situations what happened to you as a person?* I don't mean he did this and she did that. *I mean what did you learn? What characteristics are virtues did you develop? How did you feel afterwards about any other presenting problem? Did you find strength you never knew you had? Did you become more confident?* Think about some of the most difficult situations you have had to overcome. The ones where you literally didn't know if you were going to get out alive, unscathed or even in your right mind. And more commonly one where you may have had a mental breakdown, and the breaking down of the old you created a stronger more resilient, wonderfully grateful new you blessed enough to recover fully.

In all of these situations finding and developing the self is the most important way to grow. So many people talk about self-development and whether they should bother with it but look at if from a different perspective. ***Are you the same person you were ten years ago? Yes? No? Maybe?*** *If not then you have been through some kind of self or personal development.* You have begun to get to know yourself with a different or deeper understanding. I get it.....there are so many of these books out there that don't resonate with you at all or talk about fixing (you) the broken pieces. I have read and studied many of these books for the past two and a half decades. I was trying to fix the so-called *'broken pieces'*. I was living a life of comparison and inadequacy. I was talking to myself in a totally self-loathing way and non-worthy way. I was embarrassed, ashamed and felt like myself and my life so far was a huge mistake and I would *never be good enough.* ***Any of this sound familiar to you?*** The key to understanding the self is to be honest. Look at the good, the bad and the ugly. ***Who said you were broken?*** I now celebrate the life I once hid because everything I have ever been through was for a wonderful reason. Everyone who has ever hurt me, loved me and *everything in between* has taught me a life lesson. ***What have your life lessons taught you? What difficult lesson are you now glad you experienced?*** All development is paramount. The struggles as a child, the damage others, and I inflicted on myself. They were all learning. Loving people more than I loved or valued myself was a lesson in self love and care years later. Becoming a single parent taught me a deeper level of resilience and self-sufficiency. Going to university in a predominantly white area in Devon in the early 1990's when I was born/ lived in Hackney, London (a predominantly black area at the time and one of the poorest boroughs) taught me how to be more flexible and adaptable when often being one of a few black people wherever I went. Throw into the mix, I was the first person in my family to go to university. That taught me that hard work and focus could achieve big results. I hadn't done A Levels because I didn't have the standard 5 GCSE A-C's. I had three. I had to go in via an alternative route by doing an Access course which was extremely intense and full-time for a year, but got you into university as two A levels equivalent. **What have you learnt over the years?** *List at least five situations and what skills, characteristics you learned or improved.* It is so useful to reflect on your life and doing this often only expands our knowledge of our self on a deeper level.

In order to grow we need to develop. Personal development in essence is about looking at your thoughts, behaviour and actions. Exploring and ultimately learning how to master your thoughts is the starting point for overcoming any adversity in your life. I'll give you an example. When I first started this book I wondered who would read it. Would I give you something of value? and would anyone be interested? All of the common fears I'm told. I then decided to write it. I became more focused and vocal as i started the newsletter, blogs and began to share the story of how in EMPOWER 7 came about and why I believe I was gifted this work. I have had chest infections, pneumonia, health challenges, tests, legal Witness in a case with my local authority (with many other parents of children with Special Educational Needs and Disabilities) at the High Court, been campaigning, on marches, meetings with school/ LA about SEN provision concerns, funerals, two close friends becoming seriously ill, Family health concerns etc... you get the picture. I could have said 'right that's it forget about writing the book it's all too much'. I eventually decided to get a project manager to help me scale back all of my other projects so that this could get finished this year and write as and when I could until a daily routine occurred. She does have a quote in this book and was by far my best investment last year. My old mindset and thoughts would have said *stuff this is never going to happen* and list everything that happened to stop this from being completed. This new mindset of the past six years is like *when the book is finished it will be used to help support thousands of other women on their journey to overcoming any adversity using the 7 steps.* Throughout the whole process I have had to look at my behaviour and analyse my actions too. It's a daily balancing act. **So what is it you want to achieve and life keeps getting in the way?** We all have challenges, some more than others and some can also be life-threatening. I have been blessed to meet some amazing people and I tell you most of it has been down to the change in my thoughts, behaviour and actions. I was the hurt child who distrusted most people and my favourite words up until I was in my late thirties was *I'm scared* and *I'm frightened*. My close friends can attest to that. Don't get me wrong, I have achieved a lot in my life considering my age but because I found it hard to overcome some situations I would waste opportunities, self-sabotage and procrastinate until it was too late and then say *I knew it wouldn't work out anyway.* I had a lot of learning to do. **Anything here sound familiar?**

That leads me onto why we need honesty starting with ourselves. I'm sure you know others or yourself who get really annoyed or angry with other people about not being honest in some shape or form. I personally get very upset by dishonest people and although I've spent many years trying to change that, I have now come to realise I am not the moral police and can't force people into speaking truthfully or sharing the same core values. I am truthful, honest and authentic at all times with integrity and so I believe the laws of the universe will send me others on a similar wavelength. *So why is honesty the best policy in relation to overcoming adversity and challenges?* It's simple really and threefold, to see where we have come from...where we are now...and where we are going. An example of a really difficult time in my life was when my eldest son (who at the age of ten) became very withdrawn. I had been expecting it because he had endured his dad leaving to live abroad and his baby brother dying in the space of a few weeks. He was only eight years old and a very sensitive soul and child (who is now twenty). He had become attached to his new baby brother's, had held his three week old brother after he died and seen, as well as been, around the hospital sometimes daily. He was so upset when his dad broke the news he was going to live and work abroad. Although myself and his dad were not together and he lived out of London anyway, my son still had access to him regularly once or twice a month in person and weekly on the phone. This was a devastating blow for him. I had a number of choices as a mother and for me the first thing was to look at where he had come from and the recent traumatic events in our life especially from a childs perspective. He was a scared, upset, sensitive, whose dad was leaving, brother had died and the dad of his brothers had also left while mum was pregnant. Mum was in and out of hospital with threatened miscarriage from the first few months so this theme for him was lost and fear of loss. I could see that's where we were and decided that I needed to seek help outside for him especially as he'd become aggressive towards me verbally and physically. Reluctantly I went to my GP. We live in a society where black boys are labelled harshly whether we want to believe it or not due to various institutional factors and I didn't want to be the start of this process but my GP was great. We had a relationship where he was always concerned as to whether I was coping well after everything I had been through. My son was fast tracked and saw a psychotherapist. Boy was I on edge especially as I think we live in a over labelled and misdiagnosed society. It turns out to be the best thing I could have done for all of us as we ended up on a pilot programme from the USA instead of usual Social services support and after few months of family therapy things improved. I learned about all of the things he was worried about especially feeling like the man of the house which I'd never encouraged him to be. From then on we could see where we were going. So think about a current situation that you are presently in and take an honest stock check. **Write down on a piece of paper where you have come? What preceded this situation?** Next, where you are right now in it and finally where you can go (eg. all of the options open to you) and then take action.

Want to step into yourself and be the authentic you? *It's all well and good saying that I hear you say but how? I can hear you ask.* It really is easy, being yourself at all times, being truthful and being genuine. So many people are unhappy because they are living in a false reality being everything everyone else wants but not who they are. If you are how I used to be, that's a people pleaser and rescuer. Although I lived authentically and was myself the majority of the time, I often wouldn't speak my truth for fear of upsetting others. I said yes to helping others when I was shattered and should have said no. I was there regardless even when I should have been resting, spending time with my son's or working on my business. I was tired, not assertive and not myself but because I had years of experience being like this it was a habit. **Are you being authentic? Truthful? Genuine and yourself all of the time?** *If not then think about what you can* *change. Take 5 minutes to do this honestly especially if your first reaction is that there is nothing to change.*

So when thinking about overcoming adversity drawing on your strengths helps you to overcome anything. It's all too easy when faced with a challenge to become immersed in the negativity of it all but if we try to keep focused, remain positive intentionally and keep strong it can make all of the difference. An extreme example when I had to do this was when I believed my son had various undiagnosed Special Educational Needs as well as his diagnosed health difficulties. I kept on being fobbed off by school staff, doctors etc and after resorting to self referring him to a number of other Professionals he had five definite diagnosed problems/ challenges. I had to stay focused and remain positive that I would meet other professionals who would also share my concerns as I did and I did thankfully. Most of them were apologetic and disgusted that it took me six years to be taken seriously and a lot of undue suffering to my son as well as stress for me. *Not all of you will have had such an extreme situation but look at one where you have had and make notes about how you managed to overcome that.* Don't get me wrong there were times I wanted to give up. I doubted myself and was downright tired of the battle, but all I could think of was if I don't fight he will suffer for the rest of his school life. Watching family and friends failed by the system, I knew he wouldn't be able to achieve his goals if the support wasn't put in place and more importantly legally binding. Finally in

February 2017 that was put in place. It took a total of eight years to diagnose and put this into place. Patience, persistence and belief are all what kept me going. In everything else in his life he excels so this was for the structure and institution known as School. *So what strengths have you got to help you?*

In the midst of chaos anything is possible if you believe. Believing that is one of the best ways to look at the limitless possibilities. It's always important to think infinitely without restricting yourself and believe anything can be achieved. When we are in the headspace great things occur and what started as very negative can end quite positive. Much of it is our programs and conditioning as a child but it's worth remembering when, why and how our mind became conditioned like this. That way we know to 'mind our minds' with things and have some idea as to how we can change this. Always be prepared for the unknown. There are many reasons why overcoming adversity makes you stronger. Overcoming pushes you through your comfort zone, gives you strength you never knew you had and increases emotional intelligence. *How many challenges can you think of that you went through in life and said well if I can get through that then I can get through anything? Have a good think and look back on your life in chronological order it's so helpful when doing this type of reflection. Take as long as you need but you will find at least one thing.* If you're anything like me you can point out a number. Overcoming can give us strength, a new found respect for others who have been in the same situation and also be a very loud wake up call. If that's not enough to deal with, for a bit of fun the universe puts us to all kinds of tests then we quickly have to become more emotionally intelligent. For example when we often feel like screaming, crying or like we could smash things up we must master our emotions and replace those otherwise risk all sorts of problems.

You've heard the saying everything happens for a reason I guess. Well with every adverse circumstance we must look for the nuggets of learning, accept everything before finding a solution and then push harder to know this has helped in some way to shape the person we are becoming. All of these things will help us to be the best version of ourselves. It may sound quite fluffy but honestly if we don't get wrapped up in too much emotion we can overcome anything. Just hear the stories of others to see this.

So it's the belief that, *that which does not break us makes us stronger*. Resilience really should be seen as an asset. Apart from increasing mental strength and great preparation for life, it is also replenishable. By that I mean in a way that gives us strength and prepares us for any other difficulty. The thing with life is that we never know what is going to happen and when. We can make plans, goals and so forth but there will be those curveballs appear and overcoming adversity is (I believe 90% mindset and 10%

solution) therefore regardless of what happens to us, it's how we view it that has the most impact.

Quick Tip

Think about how you have overcome serious challenges/ obstacles in the past and write down a timeline (Trauma). How did you overcome that? Celebrate getting through this and skills you learned or developed however painful.

Affirmation

I AM Always able to overcome anything. This will not last long but my duty is to seek to understand the lessons within

Step Five

Wellness

" I realise as each day passes that I become more and more open to the beauty that surrounds me. Be you! Be Courageous! Be Happy! Be Alive! "

(Manjeet Kaur Nijer- Founder of Purple Leadership, Trainer and Coach)

WELLNESS holistically, Mind, Body and Spirit. Let's look at all aspects and see what ideas and changes you may want to adapt for your highest and greatest good. Love yourself!

So how are you finding it all so far? I hope I haven't overwhelmed you with information but it's important to see overcoming adversity using all of these 7 Steps from a more holistic viewpoint. These steps can also be used to get a much better understanding of yourself as a person hence also being a Self/ Personal Development Programme. It helps us to understand ourselves better and be one step closer to creating our Life by design. Something I am living authentically now. There really is no time like the present. *So what's step five about? you may ask?* Well you'll be pleased to know, it's nothing you didn't know already but something we often take for granted. Any guesses..? It rhymes with wealth..... You've guessed it!... it's health. Wellness overall is our most valuable commodity and something we don't often look at until will become ill. For the benefit of this chapter and as I am also a qualified holistic therapist, when I talk about Wellness I am using a holistic view including physical, mental and spiritual health.

So why do you need to think about taking charge of your physical health? Well as you know there are many reasons but ultimately without health we won't be able to do all of the great things our heart desires. Health means being physically fit for work, whatever the work is you do or want to do. We live in a country where unemployment and sickness is high. London being the third highest rate in the UK in 2017. According to the Office of National Statistics (ONS) the top three common reasons for illness in 2016 was minor illnesses of coughs and colds (33%), muscular skeletal problems back and commonly neck problems (18.6%), Stress, depression and anxiety (12.8%). It's worth also noting that these statistics are here just to give you a small idea but you get the point. Sickness costs money but most importantly it can sometimes mean you are not able to live life fully and certainly don't have much vitality as well as quality of life. *So how is your health right now? Anything you want to work on improving?* If not and you are on top of it in all why don't you practice kindness by sharing your tips when you see someone who can do with some advice or guidance. I know personally health has been a challenge with me for years. I had great habits when it came to eating as a child because my mum was very rigid and structured with our day. As I became college age, it was almost a rebellion. I had my first experience eating fast food in a McDonald's when I was sixteen years old (though I no longer eat there anymore), started eating sweets and chocolates daily with fizzy drinks and slowly replaced real foods with fast food and wondered why I was so tired all of the time. I also started having my first really late nights partying up to four days a week while studying and began smoking though stopped six years later. Although now twenty years ago, I don't do those things anymore as I stopped at the age of twenty-five before I had my first child. I am still at times prone to skip meals if not hungry so work on that constantly. It's been a hard battle but it took a number of illnesses, investigations and challenges to really get on top of my own health. ***Do you have any bad patterns and how to do you avoid or manage them?*** Getting into a regular routine is one of the best ways to increase your vitality. If you look at other cultures you will see how preservation of the self manifests. Do some research!

Preserving health also leads me quite nicely onto the subject of work and rest being a fine balancing game. When thinking about overcoming adversity especially when being in the thick of a challenge, regular sleep should be top of your agenda along with rest and recuperation. *Why I can hear you say?* Very simple... You are already under stress so not sleeping regularly (for the full hours you personally need) will send your body into more and more stress eventually manifest either as an illness or disease.

It can be hard to sleep or rest but when we start running on adrenaline it only makes us much more exhausted when we do finally rest. *Think back to your last challenging situation.* **What was your sleeping pattern like? How long did you sleep? What was the quality of your sleep? Did you still feel tired on waking? And in regard to rest, how much did you rest? When did you rest? and did you listen to your body? or did you do what many of us do and get busier/ more tired and overall grumpier?** There's a reason why sleep deprivation is used as a form of torture. In amongst all of this, I couldn't end without mentioning mindfulness. I know many people are really going on about this a lot. It's almost like a craze. As well as over analysing it (as if it is a new movement) but being mindful is something people who are conscious (or who reflect on self) have been doing for decades. It's so easy when facing a challenge/ problem to be immersed in it and the whole negative energy that follows, but **what about doing things you love in between? What about taking that walk in nature? What about helping someone? What about journaling or just writing out your thoughts?** All of these are being mindful, and being mindful can also help us to look after our emotional health something we go into more detail in the next chapter deeper but touch on here.

Emotional health impacts us more than physical health so beware! In this fast-paced world we are now living in dubbed the technology age we are inundated with information on both a *conscious* and *subconscious* level. Whether you believe it or not, we are all heavily influenced or being programmed depending on your line of thought. It's very hard for us to now speak our truth because the world we are living in, is almost creating people to be inauthentic. It's also becoming a world where we are getting punished for speaking our truth so the incidences of workplace bullying is much higher now. People have set up businesses to deal with the after effects of working in such toxic environments. We all know whoever we are and however we live, it's about being our authentic self and that means getting to know ourselves. Our likes, dislikes and being confident enough to speak up. It's so easy now to be bullied, whether the workplace or at home in our personal life especially as women. We are constantly being told we should not be speaking our truth because it's not about us, it's about everybody else. We need to speak our truth but we also know need to know when to take time out. We live in a society where we are constantly encouraged to do what is expected, required or told of us. In relationships many people are not having honest, open dialogue for fear of hurting others. School too, a place where we are supposed to be educated instead is teaching children to regurgitate information, assimilate into the same thought processes and then being punished if they don't, if they ask questions or have any freedom of thought outside of the box. So speaking our truth is something we are constantly discouraged to do. All of this has effects on our wellness so personally it is no surprise to me when our young people are suffering with health and more mental health challenges than our generation ever had. If people are going through a challenge they usually say *I can't do that because this will take time away from here,* and I always say to them please try to because *if you don't take any time out, how are you going to have good emotional health?* Workplace bullying is an an all time high (as I mentioned before) and many people are now affected by mental health challenges, anxiety and depression due to this. Something happens to us as a result of feeling powerless and can affect us hugely. As a parent of a child with SEND, I felt constantly bullied when I brought my concerns to my son's school at the time. Constantly being told I was a over-protective mother who may be suffering from bereavement issues patronising me rather than acknowledging my concerns, making the relevant referrals and discovering my concerns were justified. Staff would wince when I came into school and I heard I was labelled a troublemaker but as someone who has Justice and Equality as core values I had to pursue this. Unfortunately for my son it took until a new Headteacher and SENCO (Special Educational Needs Co-Ordinator) came while he was in year five to finally be taken seriously and have some more assessments and approach the Local Authority with me to apply for a EHCP (similar to the old Statement of Educational needs). I had for the most part, referred him to professionals myself. *So why bother share all this?* To illustrate a point and that being, if i had remained to be bullied my son would still be suffering. ***So what can you take control of when you feel bullied..?*** *You may need some time to do this.*

All of this in part can lead to some type of overwhelm too so know when to take time out. As mentioned before, a walk, a break from your routine, a day or weekend away. Anything that lowers your personal stress levels. What I enjoy is different to what you do so if you don't already know what you enjoy, find out! I love galleries and exhibitions as well as landscape photography but others find that a bore. Find your happy place and enjoy exploring that.

That leads me quite nicely onto talking about why mental health is your priority. Without balanced mental health we are functioning below our purpose, passions or dreams. It impacts on every area of our life, determines our functionality and certainly impacts on our overall health. We know that more and more people are living with higher and higher mental health problems. I bet you know at least one person who suffers with a mental health challenge. If you have family members with mental health problems or challenges then you really will understand the importance of making mental health your priority. It's so easy to get caught up in doing everything and not thinking about your mental health because a lot of the time when we talk about and discuss health, we're still so focused on the physical health and the illnesses/ diseases and not on the mental health which is where it all begins. *So why do so many people neglect their mental health like it is something they are too busy to think about?* **Are you neglecting your own mental health?** Many of us do until we end up in a challenging place or worse a crisis. I have never been in a crisis but used to neglect myself. When I was doing *'too much'* (work, helping others personally and consulting) I used to take little time to rest, relax or just be. I would get itchy feet and do some more (at times taking part or managing up to fifteen projects at at time). *Crazy right?* Well that was up until recently though i've gone through years of scaling back and building back up. I was seriously in the habit of multi-tasking and creativity is first nature for me so as an aquarian with mostly wood energy this *is* me. *So what did I learn in all of that?* The most important lesson, and that is that without balanced health and mental health we are functioning below our potential. Times I needed to rest or sleep and I carried on meant the quality of what I was doing though still good to others, was not my best as I knew it. It also meant I sacrificed time I should have spent with my family or things we had planned I cancelled. **Does any of this sound familiar to you?** So let me get back to the point again that it impacts our health!

At times we end up overdoing it all then end up with an unexpected health challenge. I know as do some of you. **So how could we deal with it?**

Firstly, remember that all challenges occur to test us and see if we will remain focused on the goal or task at hand, and determined. Ultimately, It's a test to overcome. First step is to take it how it is. By this, I mean look at the factual information first then try your hardest to stay focused and positive whilst finally adopting an intuitive way. *All sound a bit fluffy or resonate?* I'll give you an example. During pregnancy I had a number of problems with my womb and bladder but about a year and a half after my youngest son was born they worsened. My womb and bladder were already prolapsed and tilted due to the twin pregnancy and my first pregnancy. I constantly had a urine infections and had urgency but felt as if I hadn't emptied my bladder fully. I went to my doctor's and after months of going on, developing swelling in my legs especially and feeling extremely unwell he referred me to specialists. On my first visit the Uro-gynecologist asked me why I hadn't come sooner because it was pretty serious. I explained that I'd gone to my GP more than five times for the problems and after a number of tests she told me I was retaining way too much urine to be safe. Before I knew it I knew it they were showing me how to catheterise (empty my bladder fully manually with sterile equipment) to do three times a day indefinitely. The other option was a Colostomy bag if it got worse or permanent I may add. Can you imagine the pure fear and terror I felt as a thirty-five or thirty-six year old woman with a sick premature baby who was still on oxygen at this point? I personally followed these steps and I laugh thinking about it now but I got to the point where I could fit this quite happily in amongst my normal daily routine and the nurses words of *"feel the way into your bladder with this tube and be careful not to rupture it"* faded into oblivion. It was no longer at the forefront of my mind. Luckily for me after five months the problem rectified and vanished as quickly as it had came. I was finally able to say goodbye to sterile medical supplies, home deliveries, sterile waste removal and being on the National Register. I also saw one of my closest friends doing the same with kidney dialysis that you do for yourself at home. My point being that we adapt where necessary if we have an unstoppable mindset.

So in very serious challenges, there is a profound lesson to learn. I am going to say something out of the box but serious illnesses can actually be good for you! Not only healthwise to shake you up but on a personal level. They allow you to self reflect. ***Think about times you have been very unwell with either an illness or disease, what did you learn?*** Look back at any self reflections if you wrote them down. They can also encourage growth something I personally believe and I have seen many times. Think back to some of your most serious challenges to date health wise. The saying 'that does not kill you makes you stronger' has an ayre of truth. Challenges can either leave you stuck in a situation often paralysed with fear, apathy or a good old addiction to negativity. Others grow through the challenge, learn important lessons and find a piece of our self hidden, we didn't know we had but overall it makes you stronger and this is where the sayings come from.

Also for those of you a bit more spiritually inclined, it can also be a second chance and everyone deserves that after a serious physical illness. I personally have buried a number of friends in their forties since I was twenty years old. They never got second chances with health challenges like many of us do. I have encountered walking miracles (including my surviving 23 week son) in my life who have overcome serious health challenges and have had that second chance. Not for others necessarily but for themselves. Learning this important lesson can improve the relationship you have with yourself, others and life. Speak to many Cancer, Heart Attack or Stroke victims and you will hear (as well as see) the gratitude they have for life. Be grateful for a second chance. Second chances are there all of the time. ***Do you see them?***

It's always good to talk about healing too because as we know many people are now starting to steer away from western medicine as an automatic starting point. As we know it treats symptoms only and doesn't provide a holistic overview or preventative way when looking at a person's health. Holistic therapy in contrast heals on many levels. These different therapies from Reiki to Acupuncture, Reflexology and Various massage are hundreds of years old and are often said (and proved) to defy conventional medical science and heal the unhealable/ untreatable. Multidimensional healing, DNA Theta healing, Hypnotherapy, various massage and Spiritual healing all have their place. Finding the way you want to heal an illness or disease is your personal choice. I chose Hypnotherapy to do a lot of my inner work over the years when Counselling just didn't work or resonate with me. When I had severe Back pain after my twin pregnancy and Septicemia, I used Acupuncture and Cupping for that. I have (like you will) have to find what resonates with you at the time. I can suggest but without hearing your personal story or what problem you are trying to resolve it's difficult. My advice would be to try a range of therapies. Do your research and you will find what you need to do. It is a personal choice. As a qualified holistic therapist for sixteen years I personally would have a free thirty minute consultation with the potential client. From there we would find out health challenges, problems, backstory and possible solutions. My suggestion is to try to see a qualified therapist (preferably registered is even better) who is fully insured to discuss your concerns. Please *don't* get into block booking sessions unless you are completely sure.

So when talking and thinking about wellness, it would be such a shame if we forgot to talk about our social life. All work and no play creates stress over time. So if you work hard try to play as hard. This is all about balance and for many of us we struggle to get that balance. Personally at the age of 28 it's as if I stopped most social activities. I still had a few good friends and used to say yes to about 10% of invitations but overall I was quite reclusive and almost every evening I would be home. I would often be in bed by 7.30pm though didn't go to sleep until about 11pm and didn't have much visitors. Maybe some of the mothers can relate to this. I would spend the other 90% parenting and doing my voluntary work and home afterwards if not with my sister or Mum. I guess single parenthood does that to you sometimes. I have since had to learn to have a much more sociable lifestyle especially the last ten years and I'm somewhat healthier amongst my challenges. *Take five minutes and think about or write down how much fun (non-family/ non-work though I know that you enjoy that too) you have daily or weekly in your life?* **Who are you good friends? Do you say yes to social gatherings at times when you feel like saying no.?** It is important to do and we don't realise the benefit until after the event.

Equally important in order to stay well, we need as humans to enforce boundaries in all relationships we have whether with family, friends, work and sometimes even strangers. Create a culture for healthy boundaries. Boundaries create respect and help us to stay balanced. It can be a hard task setting boundaries (something I know from personal experience) but you really will reap the rewards In the end. I used to be available to everyone who needed me every waking moment, and this was something I did for many years consistently from of the age of about sixteen until about six years ago. It was a pattern and I was known as a community godmother which I loved on one hand, but didn't on the other because it meant others saw me as not needing any help myself or rest. Apparently that's the Superwoman syndrome. Now it's quite amusing but then it was frustrating. As I now have the balance, I realise this new way is vital in order to avoid exhaustion. I was constantly exhausted and burning the midnight oil listening to people's problems and going above and beyond to fix them, solution find or rescue. ***Any of that sound familiar? Anything you need to change or adapt in regard to that.?*** *May just be that time to have an honest look.*

So as you can see it's tricky to find balance in a busy, noisy, chaotic world but following a few simple rules imposed with a bit of self-discipline can really help. Boundaries should be number one with adequate rest. Earlier in the chapter I mentioned recharging and recuperation. Work, rest and play in equal quantities. Life is a dance and our job is to try not to overdo things by balancing. *Do you know the days when you have a burst of energy and then you are exhausted after? or if like I was, would work, work, work, help others, do voluntary jobs and then become so unwell everything would come to a standstill and be forced to stop?* A rude awakening from the universe about how important rest is in between all of this other stuff. So many of us do it, and as women we are constantly taught that *not doing* means we are either lazy or selfish but everything in moderation.

Knowing when you're tired and when you need to stop is about listening to your body and no one knows your body like you do. If you don't know your body (and some don't due to the over reliance on doctors), then please take some time to discover. It's so useful for understanding what can make us physically ill as well as happy, fulfilled and beyond tired, bordering on self induced illness (colds,flu, viruses) due to being completely run down. Health is your priority and all else comes after. Similarly, I couldn't talk about health as a woman without mentioning sexual health. As women we must try not to share space with someone who mistreats or abuses us. I know what a delicate subject it is but I am meeting more and more women who are being abused by partners and more are also being forced into having sex (which is rape) and suffering mentally, as well as an array of gynaecological problems. If (like me) you believe everything is energy, then you will know that our sacred womb and all the organs in close proximity are sensitive to energy. Any abuse to us or our sexual organs causes imbalance in the body and mind. Look it up and research it. For this reason alone, wellness must include our whole self. It's also worth remembering that if you have experienced any sexual trauma please seek some kind of help (traditional or holistic) as the effects can last for years if not a lifetime!

And finally whatever happens in your life it's always good to express yourself. I personally use daily journaling as a way to write out all of my thoughts and gain clarity and you've heard me mention it a lot. Honestly the effects of writing are not pushed

82

enough in our society especially as we are so overloaded. And as mentioned it can literally save your life. There is much research on this and the benefits journaling has on both mental and spiritual health. Again something to research. Journaling allows you to write down your thoughts honestly. At times we would never speak what we write but this in itself can be so freeing. We can brain dump, write, doodle or do spidergrams whatever resonates with you. It is another way for you to explore if you don't already do it. Remember it can always be destroyed if you want but it's better to get the thoughts out rather than having them swim around...mutate...escalate or overpower you. Sometimes we can become mentally overwhelmed and we can use journaling to write about negative emotions giving them a safe exit rather than get annoyed with loved ones and spit out venomous words that you later regret. *So where are you now in the whole wellness journey? Anything you want to work on?* *Now's a good time to make notes and have an honest reflective look. Spend ten minutes using a timer doing this.*

Quick Tip

Write down all the things you need to work on for better health using the mind, body, spirit categories. Choose one from each category that is not good for your health and find ways to change it so it becomes permanently eradicated.

<u>*Affirmation*</u>

I AM going to honour my health as much as I honour every other area of my life until it takes priority. I Love myself enough to live well mentally, physically and spiritually.

Step Six

Emotional Intelligence

" The older I get, the less of a Perfectionist I am or I become"
(Daljit Kaur Chhokar- Fashion Designer, Content creator and YouTuber)

EMOTIONAL INTELLIGENCE the way you in which you Communicate with others, says a lot about who you are. By being aware of how you control, express and handle your emotions in various situations will determine the series of events that follow.

So welcome to chapter six. Congratulations on making it here. A large amount of people have lost momentum and have put aside the book to get busy with life by now finding it all too much to do. Remember neither is correct. Everything and everyone at their own time. We are all individuals and sometimes things are harder to deal with. When the time is right for you you will know so trust the universe. *So what is emotional intelligence and why do we need it?*

Emotional intelligence simply put, is the ability to identify and manage your emotions. For the purpose of this chapter I you may see me refer to it as E.I. I'll answer the question people have asked me which is *'what has it got to do with overcoming adversity or challenges?'* My response is a lot! So let's start with an example, someone does something to make you angry and in turn it ends up ruining your whole day. You're angry with them, angry with people who have nothing to do with it, maybe angry with yourself therefore your behaviour is affected too. The *bad day* scenario. **Sound familiar?** I know because I lived in this for years. It's a negative cycle that can be hard to break. I would quite honestly say things in the heat of the moment and react sometimes so out of my general character and nature I'd shock myself. I'd get caught up in other's emotions, angry, hurt, upset and as they saying goes *you can't fight fire with fire.* Now maybe as I've aged and matured, I try to avoid all the unnecessary raising of my blood pressure, emotions and negative spiral that can sometimes happen. ***Ever have that feeling that you are out of control in a situation?*** I don't mean every now and again, I mean regularly when you can't control your mouth, behaviour or sometimes self physically. People who are not able to control their emotional intelligence are often found saying *he or she made me do it* and often blaming others, but E.I is needed in all areas of life so it is paramount you take charge. **Why?** Because all personal and professional relationships are affected by your emotional intelligence. Remember that email or text that really angered you? and although that person may have been wrong to send it to you in the first place, you responded in a way you wouldn't normally if you were not emotionally triggered. **Think of anything you may need to adapt for yourself?** If not, you will have already either be on a personal development journey or genuinely not in the mind space to reflect or change. Either way as I said, this book is a guide but all our journeys are personal to us.

That leads me quite nicely onto talking about why facing our fears are paramount in order to transform. Fears and emotional intelligence intertwine at times so it's only right I touch on this too. Facing our fears and tackling them head on, in turn breaking through them, increases our confidence, raises the bar and makes us stronger. We will look at them individually now. *Increases confidence...?* Yes it does. Think about something you are really scared of doing..... How it felt. *Got that?* Before you did it you may have been nervous, scared, unsure if you could do it and play some kind of story out in your head. Adrenaline pumping, heart racing physical, as well as mental symptoms. Then you pushed through the fear and did it anyway. Whatever *it* was. **How did you feel? Did it increase your confidence? make you proud? elated? on cloud nine? And if so, didn't that make you think 'wow if I can do that I can do anything'?** I remember n the year 2000 it felt like such a significant year to me. I decided to go to Egypt (mentioned in an earlier chapter). I had dreamt about it as a child and the trip was life changing. I achieved something I not only never dreamed of whilst there but something I will never forget. I can't remember how the conversation started but knew that we were going to Mount Sinai. The area is where an old Monastery was and is frequented by Christians on pilgrimage. They climb the mountain as it is said that is where the Burning Bush is where Moses received the Ten Commandments. I was horrified...climb a mountain..? Not only was I still in devastation from the relationship breakdown (I had been a single mum for eighteen months and my son had just turned two years old) but I was also severely overweight and worse still, had little stamina and was in a place of darkness more than light, negativity more than positivity and a severe case of historical of self doubt. How on earth was I going to do this when I was the oldest in the group and the unfittest. I heard the others in the small group of nine talk about their adventures, climbs and feelings of complete inadequacy increased over the days leading up to the event. *What have I got myself into?* Nerves overtook me and I started questioning and reaffirming why I shouldn't have come in the first place. Fast forward, I put on my walking shoes and fleece as I knew once sunset went down when we reached the summit the temperature dropped drastically. I did the climb. It went on for a few hours and just as you get near to the summit there are stairs to reach the peak. That amounted to about another thirty minute to one hour climb. I was already suffering with altitude sickness and had a terrible headache but knew I couldn't complete that so stayed with a local guide while the group continued. I was devastated and felt like a complete failure. I saw the wonderful pictures of them at the top. As they waited for sunset above (out of my sight) I watched with complete strangers. I was also the only woman and felt a little bit unsafe but still I pushed through trusting the universe despite all we had been warned of. I now use that as an example of pushing through my first major nightmare/ challenge outside of my comfort zone. I am proud I attempted it and did as much as I could, because I was advised to turn back halfway through due to the sickness but my group pushed me through to my complete maximum before it became unsafe and the doctor we had said I must stop. That made me mentally and physically stronger,as well as, reminding me to raise the bar on what I think I am capable of. *Anything you have done come to mind? Think about something you thought you couldn't do and what happened to you when you did it. What did you learn about yourself?* *Without facing your fears head on you can't overcome.*

So how can you control your emotions regardless of the situation? As many of us say but don't practice, stay calm. You are the controller of your emotions and the sooner you realise that the better. No one but you controls the way you feel or behave no matter how hard you may want to convince yourself. I used to be completely fascinated and in awe by spiritual gurus, especially those who would say you are the controller of everything in your life. Dr Wayne Dyer was a prime example. A fascinating man, very humble and open about how he became open enough to explore and develop self mastery and spirituality. This is echoed by the mighty Les Brown both of which are my favourite speakers. No one or nothing can control your emotions but you. Sometimes when we are going through adversity, depending on the situation it is also important to be reminded you may need to assess for danger. A prime example of this is if you are around someone who has a volatile temperament and explodes at times. Getting angry in the mist of an angry (bordering possibly physical) altercation can be dangerous as you know. So staying calm is one of your trusted friends. Nurture that in you and look at the situation afterwards away from the environment. It may be a situation like an abusive relationship that you may need to leave.

So building on that, putting yourself in other people's shoes is beneficial to your own growth. The first thing it does is increase empathy. Sometimes people may talk flippantly about situations but go one step further and imagine yourself in that situation. Better still, reflect on a time you were in a similar situation and you will have more empathy. It also changes your perception, and in some people can decrease selfishness especially if they are ego driven and a lot of what they do or experience is about "I". No one knows a woman or a man unless you have walked in their shoes but you can come closer to understanding if you put yourself in their position mentally, visualising everything like a movie playing out.

We are spiritual beings experiencing life on earth, or having a human experience. I believe we are souls endless and infinite. I realise you may disagree with that and I fully respect you. As souls I understand and remind myself daily that we are having a human experience in this life. I also realise we need to show compassion for our fellow humans and kindness. It can be tough at times but when we take a spiritual look at ourselves knowing that we are microcosmic in the universe and there is a world (eg. other planets, galaxies and black holes we know nothing about) that brings us down to earth with a thump. Some people (even if you are not spiritually inclined) know that there must be more to this world as we know it. Many people are living in a state of ego and a self-contained world that by all means is a created illusion. Life is about everything we know and don't know, so telling people you know it all is very closed and doesn't allow for growth. We can always learn wherever we are, however old we are and learn more than we may have initially believed. It is when we take that spiritual look that we can have a more detailed and detached look at others, their behaviours and how they may view the world. **Have you had any aha moments yet when looking at your life or others?** That said it's important to know why judging others can also hinder our own progress.

It is all too easy to judge others especially in difficult situations. It often means we are often not looking at ourselves. Think back to a recent disagreement you had with someone and how they may have behaved. They may have shouted, said things or acted in a particular way you didn't like. You may not have handled it as well as you could but our instincts mean we can often blame others and not look at our behaviour, what we said and how we reacted. *You know when you have* reflected in that way because the feelings of guilt may be playing over in your head *'how will you apologise'?* Judging others hinders our progress because it also distracts from ourselves and the work we need to do. It wastes time and resources and we see this played out daily. *Think of someone (or yourself if relevant) and a situation that was negative.* **Did they/ you blame others? Did they forget to look closer to home? What did it achieve?** It's worth knowing that looking at yourself rather than judging others is necessary as it's here you can only make change- within. You may have been, or be like I was in a sense, trying to change people. I tried to make the selfish selfless, the ego driven humble and spent many hours at times forcing my perspective of life, oneness, universal family and the like to no avail. Now I laugh at myself and say internally *be the change.* Others will change around you if it's to be. My perception is just that, and now I see everyone is on their own personal journey. I mean I was (and still am) for many years and have only just got the majority of *it* in the last five years especially finding my true purpose. Like I said, I'm now forty-seven so I must have been a late bloomer some may say. Not really. I've been through the majority of adversities you can think of and my journey to emotional intelligence was to be a long and arduous one.

Also everything else was preparing me for where I am today in the present moment. *Can you do the same with your journey? Reflect and see why things happened the way they did?*

Overcoming adversity as we know, it can be a relatively painstaking process but very rewarding. During these tough times identify negative patterns and behaviours and finding ways to break them is useful. It is also easier than you think. Negative patterns in general make you unhappy and seem to breed negativity. For example, I used to have a number of friends who were very unhappy in their lives, jobs and all they talked about was who did what to, reinforce the 'what's the point'? and then leave things as they were. I would say why don't you leave the situation for five to ten minutes, go to another room and take a pause. That definitely avoids getting into unnecessary heated arguments that naturally can be avoided. Taking a pause is also a good way to rethink and restructure, along with reflect on a situation. It's so easy when we are having a tough day or a longer-term challenge to say that *nothing good has happened blah blah blah! Have you got somewhere to live? A bed to sleep in? Food in the cupboard? Money in your purse?* then you are one of the lucky ones, as many people globally do not have that and they are still smiling and grateful for another day.

Emotional intelligence incorporates so much and I would not do it Justice without mentioning problem solving. In all areas of our life we problem solve but especially when we're going through a serious challenge if we are serious about moving on. If we don't manage our emotions, we can become so immersed in a problem and our feelings we forget to problem solve for clarity. I know all too well what that is like   As mentioned earlier my youngest son was born severely premature. Due to this I was advised by his specialist consultants (especially when they transferred his care and cognitive assessments into our local borough) to make sure he was to have all tests and raise concerns with my local professionals. When he was about four (bearing in mind he has a diagnosis of global delay), I started to notice subtle difficulties on top of his already delayed talking. He was hardly talking at all at school anyway for a four year old and I was constantly asked if he spoke. His understanding seemed more difficult than my other son. That was in 2010. I spent three years talking, crying and trying to convince school and staff who at the time (with that male head teacher and senco) were failing children by fobbing me and other parents off I came to find out. So after having to detach a lot more emotionally, I began to problem solve for clarity. The first step I had to take was to pause and assess. Assess the situation but step outside of it. *If someone was explaining this to me what would I do or say?* Then I began to strategically think well school are not doing anything so let me find out about referring to the relevant Professionals myself. This strategic thinking clears the mind of the other useless information, angry statements, old conversations you may have had and write down notes, spidergrams, doodles. Do whatever it is you like to do to stay calm, focused and fixed on a solution. I personally do this in the most overwhelming and emotionally charged difficult situations and have found it a great help. *Is there anything you are currently going through you can do this with?*

So do you believe the saying *it's not what happens to you but how you cope with it?* I do. I do believe that we are never given more than we can cope with when facing challenges and it really is down to how we view things. This is something I may add, I previously didn't believe and struggled with for many years with overwhelm and as a result would seclude myself off from friends, acquaintances and anyone new I may have had to meet. It was strictly school, home, college, work and in bed by 7.30pm as I mentioned before. I was glad another day had passed. I viewed all of my challenges as *bad luck* and something I would endure. My favourite words in my mind was *after everything I've been through and now this. Why me? What's wrong with me?* The truth was, there was nothing wrong with me but a lot wrong with my mindset. I was constantly worrying when I know worry is a useless waste. Keeping positive as I do now, was replaced with staying negative and expecting the worst. That did happen because of all the energy I put out into the universe. The laws of the Universe were working in flow bringing in everything I didn't want because that is what I wholeheartedly had been focusing all my energy on. *Sound familiar? Remember the times you did that?* Hence why so many people now claim to be mindset experts. I am one as you are/ can be if you are not one already. Remember all we have, and are mastering is our own mindset (not yours), so all we are sharing is our experiences, tools and tips so hopefully you can get there faster than we did.

When thinking about any of our most serious challenges would you agree it's necessary to keep calm in order to carry on? Well we've already seen what can happen if our emotions get the better of us right? So it makes logical sense to realise in the eye of a storm calmness creates better outcomes. The first thing we need to be aware of is not to over-dramatise whatever the problem or challenge is. Not only does it make it harder to deal with in your head and can create overwhelm, it amplifies the emotion and reduces solutions. Equally try to calm your mind. I know it can get annoying with people saying this but it really does help. If the situation is intense, where possible leave it for ten minutes to a few hours and do something creative or different. Walk, run, cycle, have a long bath or shower as water removes negative energy. Use crystals (semi precious stones) especially Hematite which is a very grounding stone. It's also calming and helps to remove negative energy. Listen to a meditation. YouTube is great for this. I will be releasing my own meditations towards the end of this year too so do whatever resonates with you. If you're not sure as I said previously, it's time for you to explore. Following all of these can then lead you to more positive outcomes. Depending on the situation (it may still be a painful one) knowing you tried to remain calm and focused will be beneficial all round.

So talking earlier I mentioned staying calm. One of the easiest and quickest ways to do this is to do some deep breathing. Believe it or not deep breathing can calm the angry monster. I use it avidly when I need. Just takes three to ten long deep breaths in and longer out during a stressful moment. Apart from relaxing the mind deep breathing has numerous positive side effects. It is known to clear the mind and create focus as well as the physical benefits of lowering blood pressure naturally, improving blood flow, increases energy levels and detoxifies the body. All this for free and not a tablet or prescription medication in sight. *So why not try it if you don't do this already?*

So that's all well I can hear you say, but when do I know it's time to take five? Simple. If you don't already know your body you'll know when you're feeling tired, overwhelmed or agitated. If you experience one of these things, you may need to have a break five minutes at very least is needed. Rest is just as important as everything else too. When my eldest son was younger between baby and especially up to eleven years old I'd take regular breaks. As I was now a single parent when he was six months old and as I only recently left work two months before he was due, when I returned to London within weeks I had restarted my old job.

I had to rest when I could. The stress of the job meant it was highly intensive and I was working with five to sixteen year olds in adventure playgrounds in Hackney. My part-time position for the Council meant I started work at 3pm and finished at 8.30pm. I used to drop my son to my sister's then as she had young children and wasn't in work at the time and pick him up later in the evening after I finished. She lived about half an hour away by bus. I couldn't afford childcare anyway on the wages I received and child maintenance was almost non-existent. Childcare was £180 a week so out of reach and I didn't really trust anyone else apart from close family to look after him. I was out a lot with my son but when we weren't, we could be found at home. He would be in bed by 6.30pm (when not working) otherwise I'd pick him up fast asleep in his pram and would go home by bus another forty-five minutes away. Then I'd carry him up the four flights of stairs in the pram as we had no lift in that block of flats. Once in I'd put him in bed as my sister would have already bathed him and would go to bed almost immediately after my shower skipping dinner because it would be around 10-10.30pm. Needless to say, after suffering near exhaustion I had to leave my job when he was two and a half and began my full-time job as mum. He had already bonded so deeply with my sister that he called her mum and she saw him reach his milestones (take his first steps and speak his first word if my memory serves me correctly).

Although I had a job, I knew I had to leave and when I saw how little money I had left after paying everything alone and my sister couldn't commit to looking after him anymore due to wanting to change her own circumstances, it was divine timing. I was becoming resentful looking after other people's children while I yearned to be with my own child and I had been in this type of work for thirteen years seasonally and part-time. Emotional intelligence as you can see, covers a huge range of things and it wouldn't be complete without touching on the question as to *why it is necessary to remove yourself from negative situations abusive or violent situations.* A lot of the book has gone into deep questioning and reflection and as souls (I believe) having a human experience, we can only make sense of patterns. Psychology teaches us the same. The job though I loved it, ended up being a negative situation in the end. Tiredness, colds constantly, sitting at bus stops past nine o'clock at night with a baby (then toddler) in a pram was too much. The straw that broke the camel's back was being called back to work a day after my son had chickenpox as well as getting fed up with having only thirty pounds a week to live on after bills and rent was paid. It did what an abusive, negative or violent situation does, and ate away at my self-esteem. It was making me lose confidence in myself and negatively impacting every area of my life. *If something is doing this to you remember you are worth more than this and it may just be time to remove yourself from the situation if it can't be worked out for some kind of mutual benefit or gain.* **What do you need to do to become more emotionally intelligent? What could you change?**

Quick Tip

Write down three things you want to work on when it comes to how you handle challenging situations in regard to your emotions. (eg. Stop and breathe before responding, walking away...)

Affirmation

I AM going to look at everything that I want to change in my life in relation to the way I react and deal with difficult situations. I must become more emotionally intelligent for my highest and greatest good.

Step Seven

Resilience

" We are not here to fix anyone. We are here to remember who we are. We are here to set an example. Practise the principles of the good and the great "

(Jennifer Beaumont-Whyte- Radical Transformation Coach and EFT Master Practitioner)

RESILIENCE is your ability to recover fairly quickly from Negative situations, difficulties and Adverse situations. Some academics have referred to it as Post Traumatic Growth but regardless of what you believe a Challenging difficulty can either *make* or *break* you/ your spirit as a person.

So here we are at the final chapter and last step in overcoming adversity. It's only fitting that this is about resilience and building it up so that you can start the process all over again when you face another challenge. *So What is the common definition of the word resilience?* It can be briefly described as the capacity to recover quickly from difficulties/ adversities or challenges. In psychological terms resilience is the ability to successfully cope with a crisis and to return to pre-crisis state quickly. All of this will be discussed in more detail.

So the big question is **Why do we have to accept what has happened in order to move on?** My first response.....overcoming problems is something we need to get into the habit of doing in order to maintain our state of overall health and live our life on purpose. *So what do I mean by that?* **Have you ever known, or currently know anyone who constantly talks about the past?** They relive every painful moment as if it were happening now. They can often be suffering from depression and/ or anxiety and at a point in their life (with or without a job) they hate, just surviving. Possibly complaining most of the time, speaking in victim mode and with no gratitude for the good things in their lives. **Any of this sound familiar?** That was me years ago. Not the depression (well not diagnosed anyway) but everything else. I really believed life was never going to be good for me or people like me. Miracles, blessings, opportunities would come my way and I would not see them most of the time. The times I did see them I would be suspicious and untrusting as if it was a red herring. I have come to realise that building resilience is about truly overcoming a situation. Not saying you're over it and then your actions say otherwise. I remember when my eldest son was going through a tough time (separation anxiety as they call it now) after myself and his dad split up and due to dad's irregular visits (anything from once every two, three or four weeks). I was over the relationship but I was so angry every time I saw him, then I'd have to deal with tantrums and unkind behaviour from my son which was worse if he cancelled last minute or didn't turn up. My son was so angry with me for his dad's behaviour. Now I know this was building resilience in my son and myself though there is no excuse for putting children through this type of emotional turmoil. It definitely increased our endurance too as individuals but riding the waves and acceptance precedes overcoming. *Is there something you need to work on so you can put closure to it before you live fully again?* *If you don't want to right now remember it will appear again, and again until it is resolved.* Forgiveness opens the doors to everything else including liberation. It's that corny cliche sometimes we really don't want to hear, but unresolved anger is a slow killer. At times it literally manifests diseases after being in the body for years. *Resentment damages and Forgiveness frees.* This personal lesson took me years to learn. I always used to say to people how soft they were to forgive but have slowly realised it is one of the few ways you can be truly free. It doesn't mean to forget, or even to have a relationship with the person again but it does mean looking at them on a *'soul'* level. **What type of Childhood have they have? What behaviours have they learnt? Where are they on their personal development or spiritual journey? And what is happening in their life right now?** I realised with both of my children's father's are men who don't know how to parent and the work involved. Their priority is themselves and they are unwilling to put their child first. The fact neither support the children financially (though more than able as working men and business owners) means they believe it is perfectly normal and acceptable for a woman to raise children without this type of support at the very least. I have resigned myself to the fact that I can't change them but I will do the best I can personally in this situation. It has been extremely difficult but my son's are thriving and happy so that is reward enough that I am doing a fantastic job. *Is there a situation or person you need to forgive to move on? It took me years to get to this point but you can too!*

Resilience is also about nurturing each other by sharing and supporting. This is essential for your well-being. When we are going through a serious problem or challenge having a few trusted friends and family to share that with can (at times) be life-changing or lifesaving. The saying *'a problem shared is a problem halved'* really does ring true. *Think back to a time when you needed either a listening ear or support and was all alone. **How did that feel? Were you more overwhelmed than normal? Did you feel you could still cope with it to the same degree? Was you thinking even more because even discussing with someone would have been better?*** Having a reliable support network increases your sense of belonging and offers an outlet where you will get different perspectives. It's worth noting too, that sharing too much with too many people can also be damaging so try to keep it to a minimum. Sharing a problem reduces the feelings of being a burden and something you need to solve or deal with alone so look at the support you have around you! Speaking with others builds resilience. This is in a number of ways. At times others may have been through the same situation and are able to share how they dealt with it. The sharing creates power when you feel supported. It also helps to release emotions of isolation and definitely reduces the sheer intensity of it all.

When we are in the midst of chaos it can be hard to dig deep and find the strength to deal with it. *So how can we?* The first thing to remember is you are stronger than you think. Go within. I realise you may have heard this already but think about other difficult situations you have been through and how you overcame them. This is also yet another temporary situation. Nothing lasts forever and unless you make it! Tap into your energy reserve bank. Getting regular meals, water, sleep all help to build your reserves. *Ever been in the awful pattern of stressful situation, under sleeping, under eating and under drinking and then feeling worse which amplifies the problem and repeat the following day making it much more difficult to get over?*

Use the tools from the wellness chapter such as mindfulness, meditation and the like. If you are interested I'd recommend creating your own emergency emotional health first aid kit. Look it up as they are becoming popular but I personally do a range of things when I am in various challenging situations that consume a lot of my time and mental energy. The first… is to remember to eat regularly. If you're anything like me , you are used to under eating and at times drinking less water with lack of sleep. I make sure at least once for the day I do something fun and creative completely unrelated to the problem. I use meditation and quiet times more and journal my thoughts so to clear my mind which is naturally overactive as many entrepreneurs are. I may even plan a day trip or go away for a few days out of London to refresh if it is very intense and I can see it lasting a while. Everything I do on a shoestring budget so you don't need a lot of money. There are great free places to go in London and beyond too. These are all things that have taken me years to understand about myself so find out what yours comprises of. *I'll say it again you are stronger than you think but only when getting adequate rest. Mentally you need to find the 'off switch' to preserve good mental health and avoid burnout or breakdown.*

It's worth noting too that when thinking about building our resilience we look at taming any inner negative critical voice we have in order to increase self esteem and self love. By quietening the inner critic, our intuition can once again come to the forefront. It's all too easy when we are going through a challenge to keep telling ourselves how silly we may have been and replaying negative conversations over and over. Learning to tame this voice increases our confidence in getting through the situation.

This in turn develops intuition so you are more in touch with your natural energetic flow, and allows you to make time for the good things. You see, even in the midst of our most serious challenges we still receive miracles, acts of kindness by others and gifts (whether verbal or physical). The key is to write them down and declare your gratitude. Put them where you can see them and the storm will seem a little more like a little whirlwind that will end as quickly as it started. ***Any ideas as to how you can remain focused and look after yourself?*** *Take five minutes to write this down.*

In order to overcome we need to go through, under and over a challenge to beat adversity. Believe it or not it develops us. We learn and grow if we are open and willing to and it makes us stronger. Pain is necessary in life and the law of duality means pain and joy are polar opposites. Our journey is unique in overcoming and is an important way we learn. The Universe doesn't give us anything we aren't meant to learn something from. The sooner we wake up and realise that we will be able to understand at a deeper level why we have been through certain situations. Looking back on my forty-seven years, I can see now quite clearly why I had to go through certain situations in order to grow. I spent periods of years in the stuck position so busied myself being a community godmother. I was helping much more people than would either reciprocate on the rare occasion I needed help or looking after. This is the same to this day but I choose carefully and no longer pour from an empty cup. That made my journey unique even if we had been through the same situation. It's probably a good time to mention a fairly new concept called Post Traumatic Growth as it's very interesting. It's core belief is that a positive psychological change can occur after certain adversities/ serious challenges. This is something I personally believe as it also explains my life so far (Post therapeutic intervention I may add).

As healing takes place on all levels energetically (during and after serious adversity) I personally cannot write this chapter without mentioning how essential various Holistic Therapies are during this time. Not because I'm also a qualified holistic therapist myself (specialising in Reiki, Indian Head massage and Guided Meditations now) but because I know how much these have all helped me when conventional therapy didn't. I used to have clients that I treated using my holistic full body massage and reflexology but I have stopped offering those services due to not only falling out of love with them but because my biggest shifts with clients have been the therapies I practice now. I can also be more intuitive, free and every treatment I do even with the same client will not be the same. Those therapies heal on so many levels, last longer and I believe along with client feedback are more powerful with my clients. *What therapies have you had, or have you tried? What one's interest you?* *I really believe if you speak it first when the student is ready the teacher appears.*

Reflect on this for a few minutes and maybe put a treatment into your building resilience whilst in a crisis plan. (**It is worth noting that if you are receiving Medical intervention do not replace with Holistic therapies instead until you have discussed it with your doctor especially if on medication as some needs a weaning plan to be safe and reduce severe side effects. Seek medical advice first).**

Find ways of expressing your creative side is another great outlet when building resilience. It's not all about drawing, painting or writing. I'm also including activities such as photography, flower arranging, gardening, poetry, soft furnishing, revamping a space or room or anything creative you enjoy. You may know what that is, but if you have been busy caring for others or in a job that takes up all of your time, you may need to explore that further. Everyone is different and that's fine but we all need to express ourselves. Apart from the obvious benefits of promoting healing and clearing anger, it also funnels and transforms negative energy into a more positive one. It allows us to be in our free childlike state, that is something we love even if most of your life you are the serious adult like myself. *So what changes can you make here? Do any spring to mind?* Remember that creating has proven positive side effects. That's why every module I deliver on the EMPOWER 7 programme whether as a whole or individually have creative exercises.

So as you can see overcoming adversity empowers you to grow. It allows us to accept whatever the situation is from a more positive viewpoint. It makes us stronger overall in preparation for a new challenge in the future as well as promoting a more positive mindset too. Every time I think *'wow if I can go through that I can go through anything'* and when the next thing comes I seem to get through it. You must have felt the same. With every difficult situation something positive can be learned and above that, can be shared to help and support others. *Maybe now is a good time to reflect on your most recent challenges and what you learned.* **What qualities, virtues, characteristics of yourself did you have to work on?**

We need to rise from the ashes like a phoenix always remembering that mind over matter is the way to go, and we are in control of our destiny. All these tests are preparation for us becoming that beautiful butterfly and our authentic self. You are exactly where you are meant to be. In order to be able to live in our full entirety, we must remember that regardless, we can endure many challenges but it's how we overcome those that becomes life-changing. In order to live happy, healthy, fulfilled lives we need to rise for our health, well-being and healing journey to fully align. The world needs your gifts and for you to step into your greatness. You were created for greatness and I couldn't reinforce that more by echoing one of my favourite inspirational speakers Les Brown. Our purpose on this earth is to shine our light, and not just shine it, but shine it as brightly as we can. Everything we have experienced can be used to inspire others. The story of my life story so far I believed was broken (as I mentioned earlier and as society reinforces) but was also the very catalyst for EMPOWER 7 being born. I had no idea that openly sharing my story with others inspired them to overcome. If the truth be told, I thought *who am I to talk to people* but as I am open-minded, honest, authentic version of myself people understand, appreciate and can resonate with me. *We are all here to create a legacy.* **Do you know what yours is yet or do you need to take that time out to explore?** My Legacy is to inspire thousands of women worldwide to live a more empowered life that they have created by design and in turn support other women to do the same. I love my community, souls and my fellow changemakers who think outside the box.

Being ourselves to our fullest means we can express ourselves freely, showing our emotions, being truthful consistently and not suppressing ourselves. Being honest about how you feel liberates you. It's a difficult road to travel if you have a history of people pleasing. You can almost feel as if you are being selfish but it really isn't. *Think about your passions.* **What wakes you up in the morning and what do you want to achieve?** Remember Chapter two on Motivating yourself will answer some of the questions. Believe that you are a leader. When you are lacking confidence and are highly capable at the very least to lead, lead yourself into your most dreamed about life.

Quick Tip

Think of ONE way you can help build Resilience using past examples or methods that have helped you or Just as a Vision board is a wonderful visual reminder create a Adversity/Trauma Board © (If it is too painful you won't be able to do this) Then on this board write down all they ways you overcame these and what you learned? What the strengths were! It can be profound.

Affirmation

Regardless of whatever I go through personally I AM a precious, irreplaceable warrior queen. I AM capable of living a fulfilled life. Things will only break me if I allow them to. Someone is always worse off than me.

Authors Final words

Regardless of what happens in your life, accept the challenges and find your peace. Don't spend countless hours in a negative spiral as everything you fear will manifest. Instead concentrate on the stuff that is going well and on what you want to manifest. *You are the creator of your life!*

In general, I believe our lives are guided by the choices we make. Until about seven years ago I believed chance dealt us the hand but realise this allows us to dwell in negative situations often blaming others for what they have done to us. It allows us to be the victims although many of us would never have displayed this to our peers. It is an excuse for us to live in fear and replay the past using it as an excuse for not taking up opportunities. Have the courage, determination and strength to really fulfill your dreams. There is no time like the present! Don't wait for everything to be perfect or sorted out as it never is. *I repeat… it never is.*

Overcoming Adversity is about resilience building and resilience includes qualities such as emotional awareness, problem solving, adaptability, self control, self belief, support, optimism and a sense of humour. I have been through many situations including Rape, Abuse, Cohersion, Bullying from schools and local authority, illegal exclusions with my eldest son, dishonesty from workplace individuals that nearly cost me my reputation. I have also Home Educated my eldest son for two years due to the treatment of him as a Black boy and Marched, Campaigned and been involved in Activism work because of my beliefs. They have all built me and for that I am grateful.

Think about your ambitions.. Passions and dreams if money wasn't a problem. **What do you stand for? What couldn't you live without? What gift do you want to leave the world? Your family? Friends?**

What are your core values?

What makes you shut down emotionally?

What behaviours don't you like that others may do to you that creates anger or resentment? *These are things you will need to address.*

Are you willing to do what it takes to replace negative habits with positive ones and continue to walk forward even when you cannot see the light?

Try not to dominate your life with insignificant dramas.... Life is too short. One of my core beliefs is that no matter how hard things are, you can do it and you have been through worse. With unexpected situations, find a way to move forward and overcome it using any of the ideas I have shared (or the many tools you have acquired already throughout your life).

114

Try to find the calmness within. Remember even during your darkest days you can definitely provide comfort to others worse off who are in more need. Be grateful for where you are, what you have experienced and be steadfast in discovering and committing to *Live Your Life mission*. Vision, Speak, Take action steps and know that we all go through periods of questioning and uncertainty. Try not to focus on material gain only. How can you be of service? I personally am celebrating thirty years of service this year in various fields of community work which I love. Try to refrain from needing public recognition. The sooner we realise public recognition is not necessary, the sooner we will live on purpose. You are on a journey of self-discovery and that it is. Don't compare! No one else has lived in your shoes or had your life experiences. Think outside the box and in everything write, draw, collage and Vision board it out with gratitude for the journey. The sooner you have clarity, the sooner you can set about a realistic strategy of action steps to bring you to your final outcome.

I wish you luck and love in abundance that everything will be for your highest and greatest good.

I know you can achieve anything and I know the world is waiting for you. Everything I've shared is no doubt stuff you know already but know that it's always good to reflect. Do whatever you need to be the best version of yourself. *You are loved, you are seen and you are worthy! You are all kinds of amazing!*

Please contact me if you want to work further together. **Wishing you all the best in your life and remember the 7 steps**

1. Embrace
2. Motivate
3. Power
4. Overcome Adversity
5. Wellness
6. Emotional Intelligence
7. Resilience

"We don't have to be victims of our circumstances, We can be Soul Conscious Creators of our Future"

Your Sister in Spirit

Hyacinth

EMPOWER 7 DAILY AFFIRMATION

I am a beautiful woman who is honest and authentic to myself and others.

I am an overcomer of negative circumstances and adversities.

I am blessed for all of my experiences as they do not and never will define me.

Honest to myself and others living my truth and purpose daily.

I forgive those that have hurt me on purpose or without knowing.

I am compassionate and kind to myself and others.

I am grateful and show gratitude daily as this will increase my happiness and others.

Today and every day I promise to live a life I create by Design regardless of my past and my story.

I will work on everything personally for my highest and greatest good.

I will help others along the way so that the law of abundance will increase.

I will live my dreams taking all the positive from the lessons.

Today I declare this and so it is!!!